Life, By The Pie™

Financial Management

Managing the Ingredients of Your Life

J. Michael Finkbeiner BA, CGA, PFP, RRC

with Jan Dean

Life, By The Pie™
Copyright © 2013 by J. Michael Finkbeiner

Published by J. Michael Finkbeiner
www.lifebythepie.com

Manufactured in the U.S.A.
Published in Canada

First Edition
Life, By The Pie™
Finkbeiner, J. Michael

ISBN 978-0-9878711-8-3

To my beautiful wife Leslee.
You make me want to be a better man.
Love, Michael

Life, By The Pie™

Table of Contents

Preface

Why I wrote Life, By The Pie™

My name is Michael Finkbeiner and I've written this book to show you a new way of handling your money. I know a thing or two about dealing with money – not because I was born with it, but because of the many experiences I have had over the course of a career in the financial services industry.

Education and hard work have served me well. I graduated with a Bachelor's degree majoring in economics from the University of Western Ontario in 1976. I went on to get a Certified General Accountant designation, and followed that up with a Personal Financial Planner certification. In the past few years, I obtained another designation – RRC or Registered Retirement Consultant.

I worked as an accountant in private industry until I was 32, when I opened my own accounting firm. I switched gears to work as an investment advisor in 1996. I currently work for a bank-owned brokerage firm.

Along the way I've learned a few things. I've realized the best incentive to get an education comes from working hard physical jobs. And I've learned that the only way to ensure you have the money to take care of yourself and your family is to take care of your finances. I heard a great saying once: "take care of the things that take care of you". That's what *Life, By The Pie*™ can help you do.

I started writing this book on a long and boring train ride from Milan, Italy to Nice, France in 2006. Traveling on my own and having no one to talk to, I was able to think about something that had been nagging at me for many years. At that point in my life, I had really tried to help my clients using "conventional" methods of financial planning. I had taken many courses in financial planning, and I was using the latest computer software to help them achieve their financial goals.

Typically I would put many hours into creating a written financial plan for clients that would help them achieve the goals they said they wanted to achieve.

Almost as typically I would find out later they had never acted on that plan. Sometimes they simply chose not to. Other times it was some major life event after the plan was formulated that invalidated the basic assumptions used to create the plan.

I understand that life can get in the way of goals, and that those goals can change. That's why this book that I started six years ago is being finished in 2013. Life got in the way. My father died, I started a business, got married, and then in 2008 the financial market came as close to a total collapse as I ever want to see.

None of those things changed my conviction that something was missing or awry in the financial planning process.

A lot of times it felt as if clients really wanted reassurance. They would tell me what was important to them, give me some rough estimates of their financial numbers and ask if I thought they were okay.

Some clients clearly found detailed financial plans with their numbers and projections too difficult to comprehend. They simply lost interest.

It was almost like they had lost faith in the system and preferred living day-to-day the way they'd always done.

They had a "learned helplessness" that I will talk about many times in this book.

I won't accept that. I cannot accept that. Your needs, wants, desires and dreams all depend on taking ownership of your financial situation. I believe *Life, By The Pie*™ can help you do that.

I inherited from my parents a wonderful combination of traits. From my father I got pragmatism and clear thinking. My father was a smart man who found his own solutions to problems he faced. He was unique and he was funny.

From my mother I got creativity and intuition. My mother could sense things about people. She was also always making something with her hands and she came from a family that invented things. One of my greatest wishes now is that she will see my "invention" of *Life, By The Pie*™ completed. I still regret my father didn't live long enough to see it finished.

I rely on the pragmatism I got from my father and the creativity and intuition I got from my mother to figure out the best course of action whenever I'm faced with life decisions.

Some time ago I had someone working for me who was underperforming. I hired a business coach to observe the situation and come up with a recommendation as to what I should do. After a couple of weeks he told me that I should fire this employee.

I thought about – or more precisely – I agonized over that advice. The intuition I inherited from my mother allowed me to sense the incredible goodness in this employee. I knew that he worked hard, but lacked confidence. The pragmatism I got from my father showed me there were ways I could mentor this person to help him perform better at work. By combining intuition and pragmatism, I was able to determine a solution.

In my follow up interview with the consultant, I told him that I was going to fire someone. I fired him and I never used him again. Like my father I used my own unique way of solving the problem. I also inherited his big German hard head.

That employee is doing very well in his chosen field today.

I've also been lucky enough to have a career in sports that has lasted over 40 years at a fairly high competitive level. The sport of javelin throwing isn't terribly popular in Canada – and sometimes I think I would've been better served if I'd taken up hockey. Unfortunately that darn skating thing just kept getting in the way. Throwing a pointed stick for over four decades has taught me that having all the strength in the world means nothing if you can't focus it through the point of a javelin.

The concept of making a Pie is a metaphor for putting together a financial plan consistent with your values. Nobody else's.

The idea of putting the *Life, By The Pie*™ concept into words and making it accessible to people has driven me for years. That has to be true or I would have quit a long time ago.

Then again, timing is a curious thing. If I had finished *Life, By The Pie*™ five years ago it would have been a good book with good advice. But it wouldn't have the online support it has now. Back then only big banks had the resources to ensure a website was truly secure.

The *Life, By The Pie*™ website makes using this system a lot easier. The site is encrypted and secure so it's safe for you to record financial data without worrying it will be compromised. Five years ago, that wouldn't have been an option.

I'm hoping I can make this book a fun and effective way to inspire you to take action. Inaction due to fear or lack of knowledge is a form of learned helplessness. Anything I can do to make you move forward and free you from the financial paralysis you're currently experiencing, I'll consider a success.

Then again, it's not my Pie – it's yours.

Please see the **Activate Your Free Life, By The Pie Account** section at the end of this book for your **free calendar year access** to the *Life, By The Pie* website (www.lifebythepie.com), where you can access the *Life, By The Pie* program and the Daily Dish Mobile application at any time.

Introduction

Life, By The Pie™ is for everyone who can't quite figure out where their money goes every month. You think you should have more to show for all your hard work.

The less money you make, the simpler it is to handle. When all you can do is cover essentials like rent, food, and transportation, there's really not much to decide.

There's nothing exciting about just paying bills. I think there's more to us than wanting to just get by.

Do you ever wonder how other people manage to go on vacations, buy a statement car, or afford a house? You question what the hell you're doing wrong. You have disposable income – the problem seems to be that it's "disposed" before you get to decide where it should go.

Maybe you've taken advantage of credit. It seems like banks and stores and corporations are literally throwing credit cards and lines of credit at you. Has credit taken advantage of you?

How much debt are you currently carrying? Some of the people you envy are doubtless in hock to the eyeballs. Believe me – this will catch up to them soon enough. I know this from years of financial planning. But there are others who are solvent, and living a life of true taste. So how do they do it? And why can't you?

Life, By The Pie™ explains first where your money is going and why. There's nothing wrong with having a latte, or treating yourself to something you want, unless that behaviour is stopping you from doing what you really want.

Why did I choose a pie to make the central theme of this book? A pie is easy to understand and timeless. Everyone understands slices and portions. There are many aspects to a pie that help me to communicate key points in this book more effectively. On the *Life, By The Pie*™ website, we have given the classic and boring pie chart new life. Using icons that are easy for most people to relate to, we can present financial data in a meaningful and effective manner.

The program itself is simple and easy to use on a computer or mobile device.

If you want the money you earn to create the life you want – a life to your taste, then this book is for you.

We're going to show you, step by step, how to identify what you need to be happy on your terms – and how to get it.

Chapter 1 is going to show you the problems with traditional financial planning. Chapter 2 will talk about the consequences of not taking ownership of your finances. You may think you're leaving your future up to fate but in reality you're condemning yourself to mediocrity. How basic human needs tie in to spending is the gist of Chapter 3.

Chapter 4 will explain the financial components of your Pie and how that categorizes your expenses. This is a different way of seeing where your money goes. In Chapter 5 we'll discuss some techniques that will help you move toward your financial goals, as well as the traps, like advertising, that might sabotage your efforts if you're not aware. Chapter 6 talks about how single purchases that meet multiple needs can confuse your sense of financial direction. When needs piggyback on each other, their power over your behaviour can increase dramatically. Making sure you stay on track and do what is in your long-term best interest is possible if you're aware of those traps.

Finally in Chapter 7, we'll talk about how baking Pies helps you learn more about what you really want. Using *Life, By The Pie*™ allows you to figure out the real cost of financial decisions – that's the money you'll pay, plus the impact your choice has on other potential choices and options. That's real power, and you'll see a great example of it in a piece written by a fellow financial planner who went through the same disillusionment that I did. He too concluded that traditional financial planning just wasn't helping many clients. You'll be able to read how he found *Life, By The Pie*™ concepts made it easier for him to control his finances. Eventually he was using *Life, By The Pie*™ to predict what lifestyle changes he would have to make when he and his wife had a child, and considered buying a new house.

I mentioned in the Preface that part of the reason I didn't finish this book earlier was because of technology. It's only in the last few years that truly secure online interactions were possible for someone like me – who doesn't have a major corporation footing the bill.

The *Life, By The Pie*™ website at www.lifebythepie.com is like an online journal for your finances. Except this journal integrates your expenses into a big-picture view even while you're adding small items like lattes at work. It takes the place of laborious worksheets and calculations. By showing you exactly where your money is currently going, it allows you to decide what changes you want to make, and it can help you figure out your financial goals.

It's also completely private. If you don't want anyone else to see your Pie, that's your choice. If at some point you do want to show a financial advisor how you're handling your money, you can choose to allow that advisor as much or as little access as you wish.

I believe the combination of this book which explains the concept of *Life, By The Pie*™ and the website are the keys for you to unlock your financial potential.

Instead of living paycheque to paycheque and never quite having the cash to do what you really want – whether that's climb Everest or buy a house in the "burbs" – we'll show you that living *Life, By The Pie*™ can help you realize long and short term goals.

What do you want?

First, let's look at what some common, and maybe not so common, dreams and goals cost.

Say you want to buy a house. The cost depends on what you want and where you want it. A five-bedroom 2,500 square foot house for $200,000 is on the market somewhere, but likely not where you want to live. If you're not prepared to live in a small town and commute a couple of hours each way, you're going to pay big bucks. A one-bedroom condo in a luxury building in downtown Halifax will set you back a minimum of $250,000 with monthly maintenance fees that can hit $400.

If you're looking for a three-four bedroom detached home in the Toronto area, you're easily looking at more than $700,000. If that house is in Vancouver, you're probably looking at $900,000 and up.

You'll need a down payment, and you'll be making mortgage payments that will take up a lot of your income for the next decade at least. Just how much of your income you want to commit to a mortgage depends on a lot of factors; we'll talk more about that in Chapter 4.

If you're looking to buy a car, you could go with a Honda Civic. It's one of the top entry level vehicles because the price is right at just under $16,000. A Civic hybrid bumps the price another $8,000. When you tack on the cost of insurance, gas, and maintenance, you'll need another $300 a month.

If your dream car is sportier, a 2012 Jaguar XF will run you $60,000 to $89,000. That will also mean more money for insurance, gas, and maintenance.

Investing in yourself is a good strategy, but it takes cash, and it might be years before you see a real return on that investment. If you want an MBA from the Ivey School of Business at the University of Western Ontario, it's going to run you $95,000 for the year – even if you continue working while you're studying.

Love may be free, but if you want to get married, it will cost you. The average cost of a wedding in Canada now ranges between $20,000 and $30,000. If you're out for something exotic, think a heck of a lot higher.

A lot of people dream of someday having a child or two. *Moneysense Magazine* estimated the total cost to raise a typical child to age 18 (until the day before his or her 19th birthday) at just under $250,000. If your child has special needs or you want him or her to attend private school your costs can skyrocket.

If your child is gifted athletically, I hope for your sake the athlete isn't a hockey goalie. But no matter the sport, the cost of equipment, special coaching, and travel to international competitions is going to be very high. And at this point we haven't even mentioned the cost of post-secondary education.

Maybe your dreams are more exotic and climbing Everest is on your bucket list. Risking your life to stand atop the summit of the earth's highest mountain will run you anywhere from $40,000 to $110,000 – and that doesn't guarantee you'll make it to the top, or more importantly, make it home again.

Just as exotic (but a whole lot safer) could be a trip on the Orient Express. If you've dreamed of the train trip of a lifetime on the Orient Express ever since you started reading Agatha Christie, be prepared. Your dream trip that starts in Paris, takes you to Budapest and Bucharest and ends in Istanbul will take five nights and run you about $20,000.

Maybe you're looking forward to the rewards of your golden years. After you retire, you'd like to do a little traveling, indulge a few hobbies, and not have to worry about money while you do it. The problem is that while we're living longer, fewer companies are offering retirement plans.

Retirement is changing from something everyone expects, to something many dread. You need to plan for that future.

You work hard. You're smart. You must be because reading this book shows you recognize you need to adjust your spending to get what you really want. You want to live your life according to your true taste.

Life, By The Pie™ can show you how to do that. It can show you how to set your goals, and then work toward achieving them. Those dreams won't be pie in the sky if you live *Life, By The Pie*™.

Lost in the Process versus Getting your Slice

Why the traditional financial planning process is failing you

Major financial institutions spend millions every year on financial planning – on software, training, and marketing. So how come so many of us feel frustrated and helpless when it comes to organizing our finances?

I believe there's a fatal flaw in the traditional financial planning process. In most cases, right from the get-go, there's a basic human need for certainty that isn't addressed.

When you start any new undertaking you have to feel reasonably certain the process will be successful. Good financial plans are usually intense undertakings that require a lot of time and attention to detail. They are also quite costly if done properly and there is usually an ongoing cost for updating the plan to accommodate any changes that alter the underlying assumptions of the plan.

Many people have doubts about a long involved process that attempts to clearly define their lives when they know change is constant. Unless the planning process can constantly adjust to the changes in one's life on a cost-effective basis, it's hard for anyone to be certain of the financial planning process.

This is not a minor point. If you look at any study of human needs, one of the most basic and most important is the need for certainty. In Abraham Maslow's hierarchy of needs, the need for security comes right after the physiological needs for food, air, water, and shelter are met.

When it comes to unfamiliar situations, like putting together a financial plan, we need to believe the process will deliver more pleasure than pain. For most people, seeing a financial planner has about the same appeal as going to the dentist for a root canal.

That's why so many of us avoid the whole thing. Let's look at some statistics. According to TD Canada Trust only 38 per cent of Canadians have a financial plan. That could explain why only 16 per cent of us have a clear picture of what our retirement is going to look like. Nearly a third of Canadian home owners figure they'll still be paying down home loans after age 65. A survey commissioned by Credit Canada Debt Solutions and Capital One Canada found that a third of Canadians are counting on winning the lottery or an inheritance to fund their retirement.

In the past, most financial planners perceived three main stages of planning in a person's financial plan life cycle. These stages were:

1. Debt management
2. Wealth accumulation
3. Retirement management

My parents were classic examples of these three stages. Like many of their generation, they hated debt and always tried to have something put aside for a rainy day.

Somehow in the past 20 to 30 years, for a variety of reasons, we have become quite comfortable with debt. The classic three stage financial life cycle model doesn't seem to apply to many people today.

People are retiring with the kind of debt that would have made their parents lay awake at night worrying.

Government pension funds are straining to keep up with an aging population. Witness the phasing in of later retirement. Canadians now in their 40s won't be eligible for the Canada Pension Plan until they hit 67. This phenomenon is occurring all over the world. Countries that are receiving bailouts in Europe will be severely challenged to take care of their future retirees when they can't even pay for the obligations they have today.

In the U.S.A., the federal government has to bear the increasing burden of so-called "entitlement" programs like Social Security. People all over the world have come to expect government will give them some kind of assistance in their retirement – but it wasn't always that way.

In 1927 the federal government of Canada first introduced the Old Age Pension Act for people aged 70 and over. They also had to pass a means test which required an annual income of less than $350 to qualify for the pension. If both these conditions were met, the pensioner received the princely sum of $20 per month for $240 per year.

At the time this legislation was passed, the average life expectancy for a Canadian man was 68 years of age. That meant anyone getting this pension was old and poor and would probably die in the not-distant future. If it was discovered after a pensioner's death that he was richer than he had claimed, his estate was required to pay back whatever portion of the pension the government deemed to be unearned.

Since that time government pensions in Canada and all around the world have evolved to the point where people have come to expect a certain portion of their retirement income guaranteed by the country in which they live, or used to live.

This is a Pandora's Box that can't be closed. As governments run out of money there will be some hard choices everyone will have to make.

I believe the bottom line is that government pension plans will have to get stingier. That's going to put more responsibility on the individual to provide for himself. It's going to require individuals to take responsibility for their finances, and their financial futures.

Doing that requires planning ahead. Unfortunately most of us don't have financial plans, and we view the financial planning process like a program of deferred success at best and sheer torture at worst.

Right at the beginning of the planning process there are seeds of doubt that affect your need for certainty. They may be, in no particular order:

1. The future you're planning sometimes seems too far away to be relevant;
2. There is reason to doubt the process you're going through will meet your expectations;
3. Most of us aren't really honest with ourselves about our spending habits and goals. How likely is it we'll level with a financial planner?
4. The plan doesn't normally start by analyzing how we meet our emotional needs through spending, investing, or saving our money. It's a cookie cutter approach that assumes we all want the same things out of life;

5. Most financial plans take a big picture approach. They
   don't take into account the "small" purchases and why
   you make them. One latte a day is $3.50. If that latte is
   something you have every day on your way to work,
   you're looking at a sizeable sum.

There's an emotional side to everything we do. Everyone
remembers his first car, her first house and other important purchases made over the years. People can also tell you their favourite
articles of clothing and how wearing certain outfits make them feel
special. I like using a really nice pen because it makes me feel good
when I write something. It's also nice to be able to lend that pen to
a client when he needs to sign a document, and hear that client
compliment me on my pen. We have to examine what drives us
personally towards fulfillment. A financial plan created without
understanding your emotional needs is like a journey without a
destination.

I have talked to people who have worked with financial
planners. Some have expressed frustration about putting their time,
money and a lot of effort into a plan that they confess they barely
understand and hardly believe. Many times that plan sits on a
bookshelf somewhere never to be used again.

It begs the question: what if you achieve what seems to be
everything by the plan's numbers and you still don't feel fulfilled
and happy? I think a lot of doubt creeps into people's minds when
they do a plan. They get a gnawing feeling of discomfort. Something's missing. That missing piece is understanding what makes
that particular person happy.

People also sometimes express anger over the hidden agenda
that the planner seems to have when it seems one of the main
purposes of the plan was to sell them some type of financial and/or
insurance product.

There are other factors that can make you feel uncomfortable
about the planning process. When you meet with a planner, only

one side is revealing all their dirty little secrets. The planner maintains an image of professionalism (and sometimes financial perfection) – and that can leave a client feeling inadequate. The client perceives the planner as having all the answers, and that makes it tough to share a history of financial mistakes.

The financial services industry benefits from the myth that financial planners have all the answers. People wouldn't pay for products and services from someone they perceive to be worse off than they are. Sometimes this model works. However if the client feels too much of a chasm between how they see themselves and the planner, the process is doomed. The disconnect is just too big.

I knew a financial planner who was deeply respected by many of his clients. They never suspected his finances were such a mess that he even had a hard time qualifying for a mortgage. He certainly wasn't going to enlighten his clients about his feet of clay. The ugly reality was, he needed to keep his clients in the dark because the only way to keep his head above water was to sell them more services and investment products without regard to the things they really needed.

Truly professional planners take the concept of "Due Care" as their watchword. A planner using due care creates a plan for clients based on their true needs, not according to which services/products will net him a bigger fee. It's the right thing to do.

A financial professional treats clients ethically:

1. If clients need a financial plan – they get one. But that planning process is kept separate from any discussion of further products and services. A good way to ensure this happens is to have an agreement with the planner right from beginning that the plan is an end in itself;

2. If they don't really need a financial plan or they aren't the financial planning types, they are advised not to get one and to do something that may help them get more clarity. Sometimes they just need to get a handle on their cash

flow and/or their assets and liabilities without doing a
full-blown plan;

3. If there really is a need for a particular product or service,
   it's identified at the beginning of the process and there's a
   full discussion of costs, benefits, and downsides. If clients
   have a pretty good idea of what they need, and the advisor
   is in agreement with their choices, there should be little
   time wasted on other things.

4. If clients request a certain product or service the
   professional doesn't believe is in their best interest –
   regardless of who would profit by it – clients get a detailed
   explanation of the planner's reasoning. Sometimes the
   clients and advisor agree to disagree as long as the clients'
   ultimate benefit is being served.

As you lose confidence in the planning process, you revert to
old patterns of handling your money. You convince yourself you
can't benefit from planning because:

1. You decide your life is too complicated for any plan;
2. You tell yourself you'll be okay without a plan;
3. You tell yourself you're not smart enough or successful
   enough for a financial plan;
4. Planning is for other people.

We all take comfort in habits and rituals. Sometimes it's hard to
believe little changes in our spending habits, even if pursued consistently, will better our financial situation.

Let's look at some here and now decisions you might make.

You're wandering around a mall and see a pair of sunglasses
for $250. You really don't need these sunglasses, but you saw some
movie star wear them and they'd look great on you. You know
buying the sunglasses is going to make you feel good.

When you look at it in terms of traditional financial planning,
it's really hard to understand how one pair of sunglasses we buy

today is going to affect some financial goal we've made for 25 years in the future. It's hard to see how the consequences of a single decision could be negative down the road when you know buying the glasses is going to make you feel terrific right now.

We need to understand how impulsive decisions now are relevant to our future. Relevancy gives us context and comfort. We have to know how decisions like that are going to resonate with what we really want for ourselves. We need to feel good about the choices we make – without feeling deprived.

If there's too much of a disconnect between what you're doing now and what you want to get out of life, you'll keep doing whatever suits you whenever you feel like it. We need to understand consequences for us to properly assess our behaviour.

In golf, if you lift your head to see where the ball is going before you hit the ball you usually miss your shot. Good golf basics teach us to do the simple things. Keep your head down, hit the ball and the ball will take care of itself. What makes that form of behaviour easy to coach is how immediate the result is. Missing the ball is an immediate consequence and you look for a solution.

In financial planning, it's almost like the golf ball is invisible. It doesn't seem to matter how you swing at it because you can't tell right away how your swing worked. The ball won't come into sight for 5, 10, or 20 years.

Once we're committed to a consistent course of action that informs our daily decisions over time, our cumulative behavioural changes lead to massive change. The difficulty is you don't immediately see the results.

Life, By The Pie™

As the title says, *Life, By The Pie*™ is financial management with fulfillment in mind. Ideally it will be a mix of daily behaviours that effect change and show enough immediate results to give you feedback. It's a process of behaviour and consequence with fulfillment in mind. When we say the Pie must taste good to **you** it means that whatever you choose to spend your money on must resonate with the essence of who you are.

You can do this. You don't have to be perfect – you just have to want it and work at it.

I see so many of my clients sabotaging their pursuit of financial goals by comparing themselves to an ideal they can't measure up to.

I always found it odd that even some of my most successful clients felt they had failed somehow in their financial dealings. When I questioned them about who they thought was successful, they usually told me about someone they'd seen hyped in the media. They always pointed to someone who was supposed to have their "stuff" together. Having done tax returns for many years for thousands of people, I knew that a lot of people who looked like they had their "stuff" together were in a lot of trouble. My clients often felt relieved when I told them that I thought they were doing well and should be proud of themselves. I found it odd that they questioned themselves so much, rather than questioning the images they admired.

Financial perfection is a figment of someone's fertile imagination. Everyone makes mistakes in life. I've made my share, and frankly I'm sure I'll make a lot more before I die. I believe making mistakes gets me closer to solving problems. At least I know what doesn't work. It also means I'm human and alive.

I can remember when I was first starting out with my own business. One day I was at the grocery store and checking out what I bought for that night's dinner. As I gave the cashier my debit card, I began to get nervous. That day I had put a lot of my bank account into my business and I got panicky thinking there might not be enough cash left in my bank account to pay for my groceries. The debit went through and I think there was something like three dollars left in my account. That fear certainly made me realize I was skating too close to the edge. I was working on building my own business without a lot of support. Sometimes life feels like walking a high wire without a safety net. But you do what you can.

Maybe I think this way because of an experience that changed me when I was young. It continues to influence my behaviour to this very day. When I was in grade 9 in Barrie Central Collegiate, my physical education class was shown all the different events in the sport of track and field. I was intrigued by the javelin. I always had a knack for throwing objects like pitchforks into the ground from a fair distance. It was really exciting to have the chance to throw something that was actually made for throwing.

When my turn came to throw the javelin, it was like I'd been doing it all my life. Within a few practice throws, I beat the coach's best throw and was told to try out for the high school track team. I made the team. In my first year of competition, I was either last or close to the bottom of all the competitors at the local track meets where we competed.

It didn't matter to me – I was doing something I really liked and I was lucky enough to have my best friend Ken as my training partner. We threw our spears every chance we got. That was a lot of practice since we lived in a small village surrounded by lots of fields.

In my first off-season, my javelin broke a few times and I kept getting it fixed by the local blacksmith. Yes, I really am that old. Every time it was welded back together it got slightly heavier, but since it was the only javelin I owned I kept throwing it. I painted it and made it look real nice and as it kept getting heavier I nicknamed it "the beast".

My unique training method of throwing a heavier javelin paid off big in my second year of competition. It turns out a heavier javelin can make you throw technically better while you build up strength. When given the opportunity to throw a regular javelin, I found to my surprise that I had gained 50 feet or 16 metres of distance. I went from being mostly last to coming first in all the meets where I'd competed the year before.

It wasn't the winning that was great, although it didn't hurt. I loved throwing the javelin and I got to do it with my best friend.

That was the best part. By the second year of competition Ken and I were finishing first and second in competitions.

I still compete in the sport 45 years later. I've learned a lot from all the years of training and having to maintain a level of excellence – a lot more than just how to throw a hunk of steel.

One of my greatest joys is still watching the javelin fly and making it go far.

I'm good at the sport, but I was never great. It's what I learned from the sport that changed my life. I haven't told you this to impress you. I told you to impress upon you some things I learned from throwing that will help you understand why I believe in the *Life, By The Pie*™ process and how it can work for you.

Here are some things I learned:

1. **Throwing a javelin is about focus**. To throw a spear, you have to throw through the point. You can have all the power in the world but if you throw the thing sideways, it won't go far. They say to throw far you must learn to put all your power through a keyhole. If you focus on simple things and try to be better today (without worrying about being perfect), you'll keep going further. It may not be a daily progression but over time you'll get better.

2. **Appreciate the beauty of the flight**. In other words, enjoy the process. You are taking action on a regular basis to make your life better. It is your life and it is your Pie. Enjoy the moments, enjoy the victories and get past the defeats. Many things in life are temporary but enjoying the process and enjoying the freedom of flight (or choice) can make your life special.

3. **Any goal, whether you make it or not, will make you a better person**. I have won and I have lost many times over the years. The one constant about throwing is that it has made getting up at 5 a.m. to train a regular part of my daily life. Javelin has given me a discipline that spilled over into other areas of my life.

4. **That which does not kill you makes you stronger.** I first heard this from one of the last company presidents I did accounting work for in the private sector. As a boy in Germany during World War II, he belonged to a boys club and that was their slogan. I will never forget the time I was attending an executive meeting for the company and he asked us all if we knew what day it was.

We didn't know until he told us emotionally, "It is the Fuehrer's birthday today."

I think it was about this time I started thinking seriously about another line of work. This guy was definitely some kind of nut bar.

5. **Compete against yourself.** The world is full of comparisons that can make you feel good or bad. One of the great things about javelin is that every throw is measured and recorded. Many of the throwers I enjoyed competing against were like me – it wasn't about winning or losing a meet – what mattered was how far they threw. If they threw their best, or beat a personal record, they were happy and went home satisfied. Having a record of throws truly tells you when you've done well because it shows your ability to get the best out of yourself. Whether you're throwing the javelin or working on your financial plan, the goal isn't about being better than others. It's about getting the best out of you. You alone know how easy or hard something is for you. If you are always brutally honest with yourself and measure yourself in an exact way, you are the best judge of your own success.

I believe we all get tired of making excuses for ourselves. Even people who love us eventually get tired of listening to us talk about the same problems over and over again. We all want to do things we know will make a difference in our lives.

Compassion Fatigue

The world is a mess and that includes countries and giant corporations. People are losing ways of life. Society in general is starting to get what I would call "compassion fatigue." Moving forward, I believe society will have fewer and fewer emotional and financial resources to help those who won't help themselves.

In October 2008, the people of Iceland woke up to the news that their debt obligations totaled more than 800 per cent of the gross national product. This was caused in large part by three Icelandic banks that suffered losses so massive that the country couldn't cover them. Shortly after, property values plummeted and the value of Iceland's currency collapsed.

Countries in Europe are in the news on a regular basis with new fiscal crises. Countries need bailouts, people need jobs, and there's a lot of unrest everywhere. The situation in Greece has triggered emigration, along with strikes and riots that are further damaging a tourism industry that has been a mainstay of the economy. That only makes the Greek future bleaker.

The United States is still suffering from the collapse of the financial system in the fall of 2008. Everyone knows about the fall of property values and the pain and suffering that has caused.

In recent years, there have been massive protests against the "one-percenters" – America's wealthiest citizens. I understand the anger and frustration of people who lost their jobs and often their homes, but blaming the one-percenters accomplishes nothing. People would be better off questioning why the people appointed to clean up the financial mess were very often the ones who created and profited by it.

The ordinary people damaged by these financial collapses were not always completely innocent victims of the system. For the housing crisis to happen a lot of people had to take out mortgages they could never hope to pay, to fuel the housing boom that inflated housing prices. For every bad transaction, there's a willing buyer and a willing seller. The buyer is left with a house worth a fraction of what she paid for it. The seller hides behind fine print, regulations and friends in high places.

Remember that most of the people involved in the collapse of the big financial institutions on Wall Street aren't in jail.

Governments are deep in debt and/or bankrupt. The time when people could expect the government to take care of them is coming to an end. I'm not talking about those truly in need – I'm talking about people who are perfectly capable of helping themselves. Scarce government resources will be focused on helping the truly needy and even then there may be shortfalls as greater austerity makes for a new grim reality

The party is over.

If you choose not to take control of your life you're giving control to outside forces that will certainly decide your destiny sooner or later. The limited choices you'll have won't be pretty. It could mean having to tell your kids you can't help them out with college expenses so they'll have to set their sights lower.

We all need certainty. We'll work very hard for things we truly believe in. The *Life, By The Pie*™ process is something you can do every day to make a difference in your life. The direction the process takes you will be consistent with what you want out of life – coupled with an understanding of why you spend money the way you do.

I Believe in Gravity and Math

The true cost of losing control

When I say that I believe in gravity and math I mean there's an inevitable cost to your behaviour.

You know things you're doing wrong will eventually catch up to you. If you step out of a five-storey building, you're going to fall and probably die. **Gravity is a law and its final verdict can be immediate and deadly.**

By spending more than you know you should, eventually you'll run out of money – and that will impact a lot of other things you value in your life

This part of the book is dedicated to getting what counselors call "leverage" on you. It's important to me that this book changes how you perceive money and how you spend it. I don't want this to be something you read and discard.

I've seen the cost of losing control. I've seen it break up families, cause personal ruin, and change the course of people's lives. I believe if you don't learn the cost of losing control, the cost just keeps escalating. Deep down, you know the piper must be paid. Many times, people realize the true cost of losing control when it's way too late and it affects them the rest of their lives.

I don't think there's anything more personal to most people than the way they handle money. Some people like to flash a wad of cash and make a big show of picking up the tab. I know one famous athlete who became known for never paying his share of the bar bill when he went out with his buddies.

Look around you. There are many symbols of success that are realized in what you buy and own – a flashy car, a house with the right address or designer clothes. But many times what you can buy and own has little to do with what you can afford or what you really need.

If you eat too much, you get fat. If you abuse drugs or alcohol, over time it starts to show in your appearance as well. Spending beyond your means doesn't really change your physical appearance. That makes it easier to hide bad spending behaviour from the world. Few of us ever see the dirty little secrets that the supposedly rich and famous, or at least the wannabes, have to keep hidden.

Over the past 25 years, I've had a bird's eye view. I've done personal financial planning, tax return preparation and investment counseling with many people from very different walks of life. I've seen first-hand the behind-the-scenes sordid details of what happens to people when they lose control. I've also seen what happens when they think they're fooling the world by putting on an image of something they're not.

Every failure has a story. The story explains why they are where they are and usually why they're destined to stay there. The story or excuse may not make a lot of sense to anyone else, but it makes sense to them and that's all that matters. I've always believed you can teach old dogs new tricks – as long as you get a bigger stick. That means finding some form of leverage that cuts through all the bull and gets somebody back on track. I believe it's an insult to the human spirit to accept anything less than what we truly can be.

Here are some stories...

My first bankruptcy hearing was a real eye-opener. As an accountant, I was there to assist my client and try to get her money back from an old – and definitely ex-boyfriend. He had borrowed money from her and members of his own family to purchase property in the once "hot" Toronto real estate market of the 1980s. Once "hot" was now deathly cold and without going into detail, his real estate portfolio would fetch half what he paid for it.

What I remember most about this meeting was why he said he'd done those things and how sorry he was.

He said he did what he did because he believed the hype about real estate values in the downtown continuing to skyrocket. He had dreams of being a real estate tycoon.

I believe he desperately wanted to be someone very different from the culture he came from. Nobody around him was what I would call flashy or showy. They were just hard-working honest people who lived their lives doing the best they could for their families. On the whole they seemed content with their lot in life.

I realized this guy had a very big desire to be somebody special. This is the need for significance that we'll talk about in the next chapter.

I also realized his need to be special was greater than the bond he felt towards his family and his girlfriend. This need was so consuming that most of us were convinced he would do the same thing all over again – as long as he could find more suckers to go along with him.

And boy was he sorry! Sorry for the money he lost, sorry for the pain he caused, and sorry for not seeing the faults in his plans to build a real estate empire.

My client has never been the same. Not only did she lose money, but she lost a part of herself. He rejected her and everything she represented and believed in. He had used her in many ways. I believe the memory of that day still haunts her.

I always love hearing ads for some type of bankruptcy service where it talks about "respectful solutions" to someone's financial problems; freeing that person from those "harassing" collection phone calls.

Whenever I hear these ads I think about that first bankruptcy hearing. About all the suffering that clown put his family, fiancée and friends through. He wasn't worried about respectful solutions when he was screwing around with their money. And he certainly ignored all those harassing and concerned phone calls until somebody got smart and called a lawyer.

All through those proceedings I could see how true it is that you can't squeeze blood from a stone. This guy was truly the stone while everyone around him was damaged tissue. He certainly wasn't going to bleed anymore. Yet he was still looking for his victims to give some form of dignity and respect.

I think we should look beyond what the law allows when it comes to the rights of the bankrupt. We should be taking a long hard look at the trampled rights of the creditors, and the people who believed in and cared enough to help that person sometime in the past.

I believe the destruction of other people's dreams is the true cost of losing control.

Here is another story about the need for comfort and security and how I connected with it…

I remember watching a movie on my black and white TV when I was in college. I was living in a little room and sharing a bathroom with two other students in a house just off campus. The movie was about a girl in her teens who had run away from home and was living hand-to-mouth on the street. Her friends helped when they could, but one of her few comforts was a small portable radio.

She listened to it whenever she could. It gave her comfort. When she ran out of money she sold her radio to buy food. She got enough to eat for one day, but the next day she had nothing. No radio, no comfort, and the food she ate yesterday didn't help her today.

I think it got to me because I identified with her. I had a small radio I listened to all the time and I wondered how much lonelier I'd feel without it. I went home for Christmas that year very skinny and very happy to eat at my parents' home for a week. I kept that radio long after I graduated.

When I was growing up, I remember hearing the expression, "That money is burning a hole in your pocket." It usually described me.

I never forgot those words. As an adult, that phrase has replayed in my head every time I felt regret over a foolish spending decision I made.

What have you wanted that made your pocket burn?

For the young girl in the story it was a need for food that made her sell her radio. Her real hunger for food made her choice clear, but not all the things we want have the clarity of this situation. We convince ourselves that something we want is some-thing we need and must have, no matter what the consequences.

Ask yourself what takes control of you and what drives you to make financial decisions you later regret?

Like few other things in life, money elicits a wide spectrum of intense emotions. How you handle your money is something you can't hide from the world.

It can be a source of pride and status – or it can be a cause of failure and despair. If you're doing well, everyone in your circle will eventually know. If you're doing poorly the truth will eventually come out.

I think it's useless to write any book on financial planning without first addressing the emotional reasons we spend money the way we do – good and bad. All spending is part of how you live. How you choose to exist. It's a form of consumption, like the food we eat. If we eat healthy, exercise and get enough rest – we'll probably have a healthy body. If we eat junk, no matter how great our gene pool, it will eventually catch up to us.

How we spend is tied to the emotions we associate to the things we spend on

These emotions run deep within us. Feelings aren't the result of a thought-out process. Many times our cravings have to do with how our emotions have been re-wired by some mass media initiative. Advertisers are very clever. They know how to give us the illusion of getting something we lack which just happens to be what they're selling.

Many of my happily retired clients are savers. Always have been and always will be. They probably come from a family of savers. Somewhere they have associated feeling good with saving and feeling bad with overspending. They usually don't change. They can live within a defined cash flow and they are happy. It is always nice to visit them. They know who they are and if you gave them more money they would probably not be a lot happier. They might decide to give the extra money to a loved one or a charity.

Then there are people that have associated spending with compensating for something they lack in their lives. By never knowing where exactly their money is going, they know they are living a life on the edge – paycheque to paycheque – a real Bohemian lifestyle. They can't be bothered with the silly restrictions of ordinary life and paying the bills. They are making a statement:

they will never be just a cog in the machine working for the man. What rebels!

I remember hearing about a guy who was traveling solo around the world in a boat for some "great" cause I'd never heard of. About halfway through his journey, he started to run out of money. It seemed this worldly adventurer had somehow forgotten he had a wife and family to provide for while he was fixing his broken down ship. For some reason way beyond me, a local radio station had fallen in love with the guy and was helping publicize his plea for funding. Not only was he publicly asking for funds for his journey, but he had the jazz to ask for some more to take care of his family. I'll bet his wife was real excited to see him when he finally got home.

I believe everyone has greatness in them. We all want to live a life of significance. We are held back by our fears, emotions and what we have chosen to believe about ourselves and the world around us. We need some clear directions to get us out of this world of shadows. The financial future we seek begins with taking some simple steps

Bad Ingredients in your Life's Pie

When we look beyond the "why" you spend money and look at the "what" you're spending money on, and the consequences of that behaviour, we start to understand what makes up the ingredients of your Pie.

First we'll look at a situation where everything is going well. Maybe there's no reason to change the "whys" or "whats" in your spending.

If that's true – why did you pick up this book?

Have you ever noticed how little money you spend on foolish things when your life is going the way you want it? Happy people don't need to spend to make them happier. Happy people usually don't need a lot of help planning because they buy what they need, and save the rest of their cash. They also don't beat themselves up a lot when things don't go perfectly in their lives. There is only so much food they want to eat, clothes they need to have, and places they need to be.

Some people always live their lives in the shadows. They hide behind the law, some psychobabble, or some therapist who "understands" their problems. To make effective changes we must take action now. The Pie you bake today is your starting point. This is the time to identify your challenges without running away from them.

Your Pie is your life

Your Pie is your life. The Pie based on your values is your perfect Pie. It's what you want to bake when you learn to do things better.

Every time you bake a Pie, you're doing the best you can based on your emotional and financial resources. It is the best you can do and THAT IS GOOD ENOUGH FOR TODAY.

Life, By The Pie™ isn't about perfection – it's about process. It's a continuous process of creation and consumption. It's also a process that has content and consequence. All the money you make is going to go somewhere. You will make choices about where it goes based on the needs of the day.

By saving consecutive versions of your Pie you can track your progress and hopefully your improvement.

Hanging Out With a Good Gang

I remember a wonderful comedy I was watching where a father was complaining to his wife about their daughter dating some badass dude who was hanging out with a bad group of street toughs. The mother's response was "Hector is a good boy and it's a good gang."

You probably like your gang of friends and associates. If you didn't, you wouldn't hang with them. I'm betting the teacher who won $21.4 million from Lotto Max liked his friends and the people he worked with before he won.

He was the high school teacher who spent the summer backpacking through Europe and found his winning ticket when he was trying to scare up some grocery money until his next paycheque.

He was thrilled – who wouldn't be? He knew exactly what he wanted to do. He would be financially secure for the rest of his life. He could travel and treat himself and his family to some luxuries. But he went back to work as a teacher because teaching just happens to be his passion. He was the same person he'd always been, but now he had money. Lots of it. And that changed everything.

Other teachers he thought were his friends expected him to pay their way when they went out. They demanded he loan them money, or suggested he pay off their credit cards. His workplace became a toxic environment and he figures he lost a quarter of his friends because the money he won changed them. He had to give up teaching. His true friends stuck with him. His money didn't change them.

Ask yourself what kind of gang you hang out with – or more importantly what parts of your past do you drag up as an excuse when you don't want to try something you know will help you? If you want to improve this area of your life, you must be around people who are already achieving or are serious about improving this area of their lives. You must believe you can achieve anything you put your mind to.

I'll give you another example. I once attended a talk by a famous Canadian author who had a new bestseller about financial planning. People packed the auditorium to see him. It was standing room only. When it was done there was a traffic jam getting out because it was a work night and people had to get home.

I'm sure people came hoping to change their lives with the wisdom he imparted, but they didn't have the time. They had to get home because it was mid-week and the babysitter had to get home. Hey, they had work in the morning.

Once out of that room, the spell was broken. They went back to their lives and the same ways of thinking and behaving that had led them to seek out this financial guru. They wanted to change, but they were caught in the same rut and once out of the hall, change didn't seem possible. They went back to their old gang with all its comfort and security. I once heard it said "if you tell me what your friends are, I can tell you what you are". Maybe it is a gang of mad spenders or people who want to leave their families and sail around the world.

You can't bake a Pie with bad ingredients. Before you start baking, you have to toss out all the old ingredients you've kept for way too long. Throw out those old containers of fear and self-doubt that come from your past and hold you back. Get rid of the old gang and join a new one. Maybe start one of your own with you as the only member.

Humor me. If we can get you to bake one Pie without old ingredients, it's a start. All Pies taste best when they're made from fresh ingredients. There is power in momentum. There is power in baking a simple Pie to start, and learning to make it better and better each time you create it.

You didn't succeed before because the process you were using was doomed to failure. I tried to use that process with my clients both as an accountant and as an Investment Advisor – with little success. I've set up this process to make it easier for you to succeed. If you have some deep stuff going on because of something in your past, that's for you to figure out. After all, you're the one who suffers by choosing not to deal with it.

Change happens when you make the decision to make it happen no matter what.

If you look at people who have survived crises, what's fascinating are the unexpected inner resources they tapped into that made it possible for them to survive.

Start Baking

I am sure you have a lot of doubts about starting another process that might frustrate you. You can't build any momentum if you're dragging your feet. Once you take a few small steps you'll find there is power in momentum. There is no power in standing still and doing nothing. If you focus on your fears and doubts, you will be fearful and doubtful. If you focus on the result you want, you'll overcome the obstacles you encounter.

Don't underestimate yourself. You're capable of so much more than you think. If you decide you want something badly enough you'll achieve it.

We all have great reserves of inner strength. We all get seduced by something – be it habit, inertia, or improper behaviour, that stops us from performing as well as we know we can.

A while back, I was spending time at a resort by myself for one week. All around me were happy married couples and their children. I could have sat around feeling sorry for myself but I chose to write more for this book. Every time I worked on my book, I felt better because I was connecting to my need for contribution.

Nothing made me feel as good about myself as working on this book. I didn't know when I'd finish it but making that connection helped me to feel good about the time I was spending alone.

As an old friend told me once, when it comes to life, "Inch by inch is a cinch but yard by yard is hard." Life is a process. We are always on our way to some destination; some point on the horizon, but there is only so far we can travel in one day. Focus on the process of the creation and consumption of your life's Pie one day at a time.

Many good days can make for a good life and a lot of enjoyable Pie baking.

Resistance is Futile

Resistance is futile. It's a line famously used by the Borg in the fictional *Star Trek* universe. It's also something I want you to remember when you're learning to understand what drives your financial behaviour and choices.

We need to understand why we make spending choices before we try to change spending behaviour. Later we can discuss the consequences of those choices.

If you've read this far I'm assuming you understand why traditional financial planning hasn't worked for you. So how come you're not suddenly motivated to create budget worksheets and future value of money calculations?

It's because you still link a lot of pain to the process of planning your future – no matter how rosy I try to make it sound. Experience paints that path as painful. While the brain might have trouble handling money, it's really good at helping us avoid pain.

You have to learn to run your own brain – to use the emotions that dictated how you spent in the past, as a means of changing the way you spend in the now. Like the Borg says, "Resistance is futile." It's futile to resist the pull of your emotions as they affect spending behaviour. But you can channel them.

When you use the *Life, By The Pie*™ system, you need to understand that whatever you do is going to fulfill your needs for today and the future. The process has to be simple and easy to figure out. You don't want to get lost in details.

First we have to understand WHY you spend the money you do. If we understand the WHY, then the WHAT is easy. Then maybe down the road you can look at some good reasons to change some of your spending habits.

This process helps you **identify** your current behaviour, **quantify** its significance in your life, **qualify** how important it is to you, and **decide** what you want to do about it – then take **action** and do it.

We begin with four basic human needs. How we spend our time and money is a reflection of how we fulfill and express these needs. Later they'll help us make our life's Pie. There are certainly other needs, but these are the main ones satisfied when you spend money and/or buy things.

These four needs become the four parts of your Pie. They are:

1. The Crust (the need for safety, security, comfort, predictability)
2. The Filling (the need for variety, enjoyment, excitement, fun)

3. Sugar or Sweet (the need for love, family, friends, connections)
4. Spice or Savoury (the need for significance, reward, achievement, recognition, success)

The Crust

The first layer of your Pie is the most important because it's the base for everything else. Before we can figure out a future, we need to feel safe and comfortable. We need to feel absolutely certain our needs for employment, health, resources, family, and property are met. Think of them as survival instincts.

When it comes to financial survival, there's a rhythm and structure to the things we must do.

Life has a certain rhythm and so do bills and debt payments. We all need a basic crust or protective structure of routine and predictability that gives us stability. We can't dream of a better tomorrow if we don't have a job or we're not paying the bills today.

This crust also holds the Filling. Since the crust satisfies the most basic needs, it's also the most powerful in terms of its effect on our behaviour. In the needs spectrum, there is a wide gap between self-denial and self-indulgence.

Ideally you operate in the mid-range between those two extremes most of the time.

Is a three bedroom town home in the suburbs enough shelter and property to make you feel safe? Or does it have to be a mansion on an island? Only you can know what you need. You should also question how much of that "need" is you, and how much is programming from family, peers, society and advertising.

You have to figure out if you're spending money on shelter, clothing and food according to what you need and want. Or is someone pushing your buttons? Pushing you to spend money in ways that won't benefit you long-term?

The beauty of making your own crust is that you start with something you're comfortable with. You have to be brutally honest with yourself to make this Pie your own – and that's something only you can determine. A good crust results when you move past the programming, and learn to run your own brain.

Spending to make you feel good

I heard a teenager talk about going to the local mall to indulge in what she called "retail therapy." She got certainty and comfort from knowing that whatever she bought, she'd feel good at the end of the day – or at least until the credit card bill arrived. Spending can make you feel good, but if it's a temporary feeling quickly replaced by guilt and shame, then you know this indulgence won't work for you long-term.

You buy food to meet your nutritional needs. When you use food to fill a void in your life – whether it's a lack of self-esteem, guilt, loneliness or depression – you run into trouble. Over-eating won't make you feel good when you look in the mirror, and it can cause health problems.

Maybe your yearly restaurant expenditure is bigger than the budget of some small emerging nation. Indulging in luxuries you can't afford won't bring you respect from others over the long haul. And unlike a tiny nation, you can't print money to bail yourself out.

Sometimes spending money the way you always have gives you a sense of certainty and comfort. Knowing you're always going to be short of cash can be a self-fulfilling prophecy. It could reinforce a sense of yourself as a victim or screw-up. Your spending confirms your view of life, and yourself.

You have a "learned helplessness." I've seen this and been frustrated by it many times when I try to help clients. They're the ones who always have problems making ends meet. And they always have someone or something to blame.

In other words, they've found a story that justifies their behaviour. It may not make sense to anyone else, but that's not what it's about. The story gives them a reason not to try anything new or try to help themselves.

I have other clients who consistently take responsibility for actions. They do what they can to keep financial commitments. They discipline themselves to do what they've promised.

I stated earlier in Chapter 3 that I believe in gravity and math. Not taking control and responsibility in the short-term puts you on a collision course for the ultimate in discomfort and loss of control. That's when the courts or a bailiff steps in and forces you to take actions that I can guarantee will not feel at all comfortable.

You don't make your car payments – they take away your car.

You fall behind in your rent or mortgage – you get evicted.

Spend too much of your retirement nest egg early in your retirement – you'll outlive your money.

One of my oldest clients recently died. He was 96. He was careful with money his whole life and accumulated a very respectable amount from very modest means. He had peace of mind because he lived his life according to his own taste. It was an honour, privilege, and a pleasure to deal with him.

Finding a reason for not taking responsibility for your current actions is a short-term excuse that's a lousy strategy for long-term happiness. Do you really want to see yourself as a financial victim?

In my many years in the financial industry I have been close to some of my clients in their final days. That's when all the baloney gets stripped away and they know if they've been honest with themselves. Those who have lived life according to their true taste and achieved happiness on their own terms are special.

The Filling

Only after you're sure you have enough comfort and security to feel safe can you consider responding to the pull of other needs – whether that's variety, fun, uncertainty, adventure or surprise.

Some people have a strong need for variety and adventure. Ask them and they'll tell you it makes them feel more alive. An extreme activity like mountain climbing requires all your senses to be engaged to get to the peak and then down the mountain alive.

Within that need, there's a high element of risk – the sauce for the goose – or the goal would not be perceived as worthwhile. People die climbing mountains, but every year there's a lineup of climbers eager to risk everything to meet the challenge.

To a person with a strong need for security and routine, this extreme desire for adventure seems insane, but even the most straight-laced of us has a need to step out of our routines from time to time. It's just not likely our walk on the wild side will include climbing Everest.

Once you've learned to enjoy adventure, you start to anticipate it. You must have it. The heart will not be denied. That level of desire can make a person act against reason, logic, budgets, past promises and New Year's resolutions. Once you experience it, you will forever hunger for it.

The heart rules the head. Once the heart decides, the head realizes it's fighting a losing battle and seeks ways to justify what the heart has already decided. Once the story is hammered out in some quasi–believable fashion (usually with heaps of psycho-babble), that's your story and you're sticking to it.

Once you have a Pie crust of comfort and security, you can fill it with those things that fulfill you. The "fulfilling" is the filling in your Pie. Even cavemen had to leave the security of the cave and take risks – even if they risked being eaten by a sabre-toothed tiger.

My family from Northern Ontario used to tell stories of people who worked at logging camps. They'd drive five hours just to have a beer in Sudbury on Friday night, and then drive back to camp the next day just to get the heck out of there for a while.

The crust and filling of the Pie are definitely distinct from each other in terms of their composition. They're different, yet they either work in harmony or conflict with one another to shape the taste of your life. There's no filling without a crust to hold it; but without filling there's no Pie.

Spice or Savoury

We all want to feel unique in some way. That somehow we matter, and that we are important. This is the need for significance or uniqueness. It is also the need that makes us want to achieve and set goals.

In your life Pie, you want to experience some form of spice. It may be money you spend on education, or going on a trip that has some form of significance to you. In the business world this need may drive you to having a certain job, or certain amount of income.

We all want to feel significant. When that need is strong, it can be manipulated to make you spend money in ways that have nothing to do with your true taste. Advertisers have been using this form of persuasion / manipulation successfully for a very long time.

For example, take any ad for a high-priced luxury car you see on TV or any form of advertising for cars. The person driving this car is never perceived to be unimportant or a nobody. Owning this car means you have arrived in life. It is a symbol of your success or social status.

If you are a guy in the market for a truck – don't you want a manly truck? Don't you want a truck that in the commercial looks like you can haul an ocean liner? Or take you on an excursion through the Sahara desert? The audio portion of these commercials is done by someone who must've played in a lot of Western movies in his day. The voice is deep, tough and really manly. You know any truck he sells is made for real men.

Where you live and the house that you own can also be a symbol of significance. Some people will give all that they can to live in the right neighborhood and/or have a home of significance with an address that most people would perceive to represent a certain status.

There's nothing wrong with the need for significance. In fact no need is wrong or right. The problem or challenge occurs when no true significance is really there for you in the long term. If you were coerced into buying something by some form of media or peer pressure, then the importance or significance of that purchase will slowly drift away when you realize it is not really something that is important or significant to you.

If you're buying something to feel significant, you should always examine why it makes you feel that way. If what you are buying is only going to make you feel good on a temporary basis and you will soon have to go out and buy something again to feel good, it may be time to start asking yourself some hard questions.

It might feel really good at the time to spring for a $500 haircut with the stylist de jour, but that has no long-term benefit and cannot be considered something that has a true significance. In the context of *Life, By the Pie*, it is not a true taste for your Pie and it won't nourish you.

Sugar or Sweetness

We all feel the need for connection – to someone special, to a family, and usually to a larger community whether that's religious, social, or an institution.

This need to connect is powerful. It drives us to join clubs, gangs, be part of a team, or hang out with the people with whom we work. And just like in the song "You're nobody 'til somebody loves you," we all need to belong to a special someone. We all want someone to love who loves us. Someone you feel a special connection to.

You can spend a whole lot of money satisfying that need to connect. It might start with club dues, membership to a golf club, or season tickets.

To show you're part of a select social or economic set you might be paying out big bucks to put your child in the right school, and eventually the right Ivy League college.

Think of all the soccer moms who have to have just the right vehicle to drive the kids. This powerful need makes the quality and safety rating of the vehicle she uses of utmost importance. The vehicle not only drives these kids, but also must protect them – just like she does.

Just how highly we value our connections becomes apparent when we're under financial stress.

The 2008 recession pushed a lot of rich yuppies to the financial brink. They had some tough decisions to make. As their cash flow dwindled and their debts were mounting, they had to pick and choose what they truly valued.

According to media reports about yuppies in Toronto, they had no problem driving a cheaper car, and swearing off buying expensive clothes and vacations. If their backs were against the wall, they would even pull their kids out of pricey private schools and let them join the great unwashed by switching them to the public school system.

However they did have a line they would do anything not to cross. They would cut costs everywhere else in their lives, but they would hang on to memberships in their favourite club to the bitter end. This was the club all their friends belonged to; the club where they believed they belonged. Quitting their club would put them into social exile and shame them beyond bearing.

Summary

Understand something here. I don't judge these needs as wrong. The purpose of this was to simply identify what needs drive certain behaviours that result in spending – both good and bad.

We're using the analogy of the Pie to explain the "why" of your spending decisions. That's all the *Life, By The Pie*™ process seeks to accomplish. It gives you a new frame of reference to understand your spending habits. Knowing "why" you spend is one more piece of the puzzle along the path to understanding your Life's Pie.

What goes into your Pie may well change over time.

The psychological needs I have described as ingredients in your Pie have, of course, been simply stated. I don't pretend to know you or know what really makes you tick. If you're looking for a reason for still hating the kid who took your truck while you were playing in the sandbox when you were three years old, you won't find it here.

The philosophy of *Life, By The Pie*™ is to give you the tools to figure things out on your own. Unlike most financial commercials, the underlying assumption here is that you really do have the ability to figure things out for yourself and do something about it.

Ask yourself why you spend the money you do. If the reasons make sense to you – you alone should decide what you want to do about it.

Find out on your own what ingredients make your life's Pie taste good to you

Most people indulge in retail therapy at least occasionally. We add a pinch of adventure by heading to an outlet mall where there's adventure in finding something special at a bargain price. You get the comfort of buying stuff, but the different venue, and sights and people make it more fun.

I remember my uncle taking me window shopping in Exeter. I was young and I just couldn't understand the logic of looking without buying. Then again – I wanted him to buy me candy.

In the mall there are familiar stores (comfort) but they might have a new sale (adventure or hand-to-hand combat to get the deals before someone else does) or they may have new products on display (surprise).

The comfort side of this outing may dominate your behaviour. You go to the mall and maybe come home without buying anything. If you were a confirmed shopaholic, not buying might cause a nervous twitch that would require serious "retail therapy" to cure.

If the fun/variety (or what the hell) side of you dominates at the mall you might overspend on things you don't really need and come home wondering why you let yourself go like that. You start planning for a regular diet of pasta and margarine until the next pay cheque hits the bank.

The trick – and I know you've heard this before – is to have the adventure, buy what you can afford and need, and come home without twitches or buyer's remorse.

Unless you're Warren Buffet or Bill Gates, the money you spend on these first two parts of your Pie – the crust and filling – will probably account for most of your important purchases. These are powerful needs that can be leveraged – either by you or outside forces – to get you to spend money in ways that put the ability to fulfill other needs at risk.

We can all relate to wanting something so much we're ready to damn the consequences. By fixating on something we want, we allow ourselves to be hypnotized by our desires. If we allow all our wants to hypnotize us, we're in big trouble.

We need to prioritize what we really need to stop that from happening.

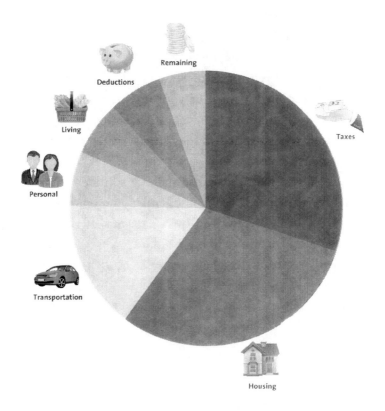

Slicing the Pie - Content and Consequences

You are what you focus on. There is no magic formula to managing your expenses. If you don't pay attention to what you're doing, things get out of control. *Life, By The Pie*™ gives you a way of understanding what you're doing and how you're doing it. It also clearly links the content and consequences of your choices.

Perhaps you experienced feelings of regret a few times when you knew your bank account was low and there was no infusion of cash coming soon. You wish you hadn't blown money on some things you didn't really need.

A lot of times the reason you made foolish purchases – the ones that don't serve you long-term – is because your focus was elsewhere. The test is to see how hard these moments of realization hit you. If you experience a lot of regret and remorse, you probably had a focus that was way out in left field and life has just delivered you a slap upside the head.

I remember once when I was about 35 still working as an accountant in downtown Toronto. I thought it would be a really good idea to buy a charcoal gray suit. All the sharply dressed guys I knew had a charcoal gray suit, so I went out and got one on sale.

I took it home and went to put it in a part of my closet that I hadn't used in a while. There, much to my surprise, sitting untouched, was a charcoal gray suit almost exactly the same as the one I just bought.

I was so focused on the suit, how everyone of significance had one, and how it would make me feel, that I forgot that I already had one. I think we all have our charcoal gray suit stories.

The process of *Life, By The Pie*™ keeps you focused on the daily decisions you make and how those decisions affect your goals and the way you want your Pie to taste.

Let's start slicing a Pie and examine what each slice means…

Taxes

One of the biggest slices out of your Pie is taxes. I think the tax man knows a lot about cash management because he takes his money off the top. (What he does with it is a subject that could be written about forever.)

I've had a lot of clients complain about the taxes they pay. I understand their concerns but I don't think the payment of tax should be used as an excuse for bad behaviour. Your tax bill is a percentage of what you earn. It's never more than your share of what you earn and should be thought of as money you never had.

When it comes to taxes, I think it is useful to understand two different concepts: **average tax rate** and **marginal tax rate**.

Your **average tax rate** is the overall tax that you pay as a percentage of your overall income. In Canada, even for the highest income earners, that number ranges from 38 per cent to 40 per cent. For anyone under $100,000 of income, that number can range from 0 to 25 per cent.

When I did tax returns for a living, I actually had people who believed the government took more from their paycheque than they got to keep. Some of them used this reasoning as an excuse for not working overtime because they didn't believe they would take home any more money by doing so. This form of learned helplessness based on an inaccurate understanding of the facts can be damaging.

Your **marginal tax rate** is the amount of tax you pay on every new dollar that you earn. If you're already earning $50,000 per year, you will pay roughly 38 per cent on your 51st thousand dollars. If you're making $20,000 per year you will pay roughly 25 per cent on your 21st thousand dollars.

The marginal tax rate in Canada is never greater than roughly 46 per cent. The only exception to this is the claw-back rate on old-age security when a retired individual makes more than the threshold amount of approximately $53,000. In this case the claw-back along with the tax can be as much as 65 per cent.

But this book isn't about taxes.

Taxes are what they are. Taxes support society with essential services. Unless you have a plan to take over the government, there is little you can do about it short of moving to another country. Control the controllable and move on to other pieces.

Every Pie has a home - housing expenses

We all need a place to live. That statement alone suggests your home is a big part of your life experience. We all remember vividly places we have lived during different times of our lives.

The size of house and its location will go a long way to determining its cost. This is a major slice of your Pie. How major you make it is up to you – and to some extent, the person or entity from whom you borrow.

When you're buying a new home you should be aware of the guidelines most lenders follow about debt levels and debt service costs. The first thing you need to understand is the **Gross Debt Service** ratio or **GDS**. This ratio refers strictly to the cost of carrying a home. It includes mortgage payments, heating costs and some portion of condo fees where applicable. Most lenders require that these costs not exceed more than 32 per cent of your gross monthly income. That means if you're making $5,000 per month you cannot spend more than $1600 on your total housing costs.

Lenders also pay attention to your total debt obligations. The **Total Debt Service** ratio or **TDS** measures your total debt obligations including housing costs, loans, car payments and credit card bills. The generally accepted limit for all these payments is no more than 40 per cent of your gross monthly income.

The Home and Debt Slice Calculator

If you understand the math of the above ratios, it becomes very simple to figure out how much debt you can afford based on your income and current interest rates on whatever loans you have/need.

I created the home and debt slice calculator in The *Life, By The Pie*™ online program to help people understand what they can really afford and how this slice affects the rest of the Pie. To use this program, all you have to do is:

1. **Input** your family income and let the program calculate the price limit on a home you can afford.
2. The required mortgage amount will be calculated from this and you must **determine** what your mortgage payments will be and **input** that amount into your monthly payment field.

3. The program will do the rest in calculating your **GDS** and **TDS** limits for this slice of your Pie.

Example One – 5 per cent Down Payment

If you have a family income of $150,000 and you're looking to buy a home, the place to start is by figuring out the price you can afford. Lenders usually calculate that as a dollar value equal to 3.4 times the family income. That formula usually keeps everything in line with all the required ratios.

Your **GDS** limit is $4,000 per month (Family Income of $150,000 divided by 12 months equals $12,500 per month. The **TDS** of 32 per cent equals $4,000).

In this case if you take a household income of $150.000 and multiply by 3.4, it equals $510,000. This is the price limit of the house you can afford.

A five per cent down payment is $25,500 and the amount to be mortgaged is $484,500. ($510,000 - $25,500 = $484,500.)

I looked up a mortgage calculator online, and a $484,500 mortgage for a five year term @ 4.5 per cent interest is $2,679 per month.

Your **GDS** limit is $4,000 per month. Your mortgage payment is $2,679. The means you have a limit of $1,321 per month ($4,000 - $2,679) that you can pay on all your other home-related expenses to stay within your **GDS** limit.

At 40 per cent of your monthly income, your **TDS** is $5,000 per month (40 per cent of your monthly income of $12,500). That means you must not spend more than $5,000, or $1,000 more on all debt.

Example Two – 20 per cent Down Payment

If you have the same family income of $150,000, you would use a factor of 4.0375 to figure out the most you should pay for a home with 20 per cent down. The more expensive the home is, the more variable the price can be. I would recommend a higher down payment on more expensive homes.

In this case if you take $150,000 multiplied by 4.0375, the highest price of a home you can afford is $605,625.

At 20 per cent, the down payment is $121,125, and the amount to be mortgaged is $484,500 ($605,625 - $121,625 = $484,500). This, of course, is the same mortgage that was calculated before and the payment is $2,679.

From here on all the numbers are the same as the previous example, but you start with a 20 per cent cushion instead of 5 per cent.

Remember, the devil is in the details. These ratios that allow you to get into a home can also work against you to get you out of your home. Lenders have very strict rules when it comes to how much you can spend to service debt and home obligations. If interest rates rise and/or your income situation changes, it could have a material effect on your ability to hang on to what you bought.

It's important to remember that having a down payment of 5 per cent means you must pay extra costs for a high ratio mortgage. It also means you don't have a lot of wiggle room if the value of your property goes down when it's time to renew your mortgage.

For the past number of years, we have enjoyed historically low interest rates. This low rate environment has greatly affected the prices of many housing markets and the behaviour of house buyers everywhere. It's hard to imagine the double digit mortgage rates of the not too distant past and how expensive debt once was.

If interest rates were to go up even modestly in the future, there would be a great reckoning in most housing markets – and in many households.

Another factor that has affected the housing market in the past generation is the new reality of two incomes to service the debt. What if one of those incomes were to disappear? Losing an income because one spouse loses a job or stays home to start a family could severely limit a family's ability to hang on to their home

In reality, you alone must decide how big the mortgage slice of your Pie should be. The term "mortgage poor" has been turned into "mortgage default" in the past five years as real estate has taken a tremendous hit in many areas, especially in the U.S. The cost components of owning a home are not likely to reduce over time.

Even after you pay off the mortgage, there are still the costs of property taxes, hydro, gas, insurance, repairs and maintenance. I've had many clients tell me over the years that they could not believe how significant the costs of owning a home still were in their retirement years – long after they had paid off their mortgages.

You can spend whatever you want on your house, but at this point in the slicing of your Pie it should be pointed out that between taxes and housing you could be spending 50 per cent of your Pie in just those two areas. This means half your Pie is gone and all you have to show for it is your house.

My mother always told me to make my house nice. She gave me this advice when I was in my 20s and first looking to make a home of my own. I think it is important to make your house nice – but it's just as important that your house doesn't become your prison of debt.

Vehicle expenses

After you've paid your taxes and paid for your home, you'll need a way of getting around and seeing the world. There's no doubt that a car in today's society can make a statement about who you are.

We all have to be somewhere. We would all like to go somewhere. Life is movement. You probably need a car.

Even if you really do not need a car, there is still a price to be paid for movement. As the song goes, "People got to move". It could be public transit or the cost of a bicycle, but we're talking about the significant cost of owning a vehicle.

I've seen clients spend one year's salary or more on a vehicle and then do whatever was necessary to keep it. I've also seen clients who were quite happy to buy something used. They were very happy spending a fraction of what other people spent on a vehicle.

I've seen great arguments supporting the concept of buying used vehicles and I will leave that subject to more knowledgeable experts. I understand the concept of driving the "right" vehicle because I'm a financial professional and know the car I drive has to make the right impression. However, I haven't bought a new car in over 20 years.

Just because you can afford a new car doesn't mean you should buy one. If the new version of what you buy is 50 per cent more than the used car, could the difference you pay be the cost of your ego?

In a few years, no one but you will know who the original owner of that vehicle was. Most new cars cost a lot more than buying them used. There may be great reasons for choosing a new vehicle. My final comment here is, make sure that reason is not the cost of your ego.

The rest of your Pie

At this point you should be starting to see the consequences of the size of your slices. Take a hard look at what taxes, housing, and your vehicle expenses add up to as a percentage of your overall Pie. Let's look at your slices so far:

1. There is little or no control that you can exert on the **taxes** you pay.
2. You do have choice and control over how much you spend on **housing**.
3. Unless you live in Folsom prison, you need some way of getting around – you need a **vehicle** – but look at this expense category carefully.

For these reasons I would call what we have discussed so far the pre-set pieces. Most people will have a significant portion of their Pie allocated to these three.

Once your mortgage or rent payments and vehicle payments are set, you are really dealing with the rest of your Pie. This is the portion of the Pie you can exert more control over.

Let's not kid ourselves here. **If most of your Pie is gone at this point you are in serious trouble!** You need to get some professional advice to reduce those costs ASAP.

Maybe you don't need professional help. Maybe you just need to give yourself a slap upside the head. For example, if your daughter cannot go to private school because you wanted to drive a Bentley, this is when you need to understand how your slice decisions affect your life. You don't need help with the obvious.

You could borrow more to get yourself through – and I know there are times in life when that may be necessary. However, if what you really can't afford is the cost of your ego, it may be time to make some hard decisions before those decisions are made for you.

The remains of the Pie - your true disposable income

Your Pie has been severely diminished after the taxman, housing, car expenses and debt payments have been made.

It's a shock to see how small a portion is left after our regular visitors have had their share. This is your disposable income.

Learning to focus on making the best of what remains of your Pie is going to be the agent of real change in your life. Whatever time frame of reference you use to value what's left: daily, weekly, monthly, or yearly; will really help you understand how, why, and when you spend the money you do. This new focus will move you to consider spending decisions more carefully.

To understand how the brain works around this, I have two examples:

The first example is the behaviour of anyone paid on a monthly basis. The day the paycheque goes in is usually when major purchases are made because there's no concept that you lack the funds. It's like, "Wow! I have all this money!!" Somehow you forget there's a long time to go before the next monthly paycheque hits the account.

The new month starts and the bank account is taking hits, but they become progressively smaller hits as the account balance diminishes.

In the end, there may be more month than there is money and you're eating Kraft Dinner until the next paycheque. Here the concept of lack is alive and kicking. This type of behaviour is really not wrong or right – it just is.

Another example of this is more unique.

When I took economics in university, a professor told a story about World War II prisoners of war and how their behaviour demonstrated the concept of inflation and deflation.

For these prisoners in German POW camps, the currency was cigarettes. It didn't matter if you smoked or not, cigarettes were what you used to pay for anything you bought from other prisoners. Unlike hard currency, cigarettes were also smoked. This unique way of reducing the money supply had a huge effect on the value / cost of things over time.

The money supply increased when the Red Cross packages arrived for all the prisoners. Amongst the many goodies was a certain supply of cigarettes. This infusion of currency caused the prices of everything to skyrocket.

A lot more cigarettes meant instant hyperinflation. If a blanket was worth – say five cigarettes before the parcels arrived, now it cost 20. Chocolate, coffee and other personal items were going to cost you a lot more because of this increase in the money supply.

The day the Red Cross parcels arrived was a lousy day to buy anything because that's when prices peaked.

As time passed and the cigarette supply went up in smoke, prices plummeted. The number of cigarettes necessary to buy things went down as scarcity pushed the value of each cigarette up. Sound familiar? This is hyper-deflation.

Smokers were at a big disadvantage – especially if it was cold and they had sold their blankets for cigarettes.

Don't get left out in the cold. Understand scarcity before you run out of blankets or cigarettes – or Pie.

Borrowing to get more Pie

The world gives us lousy examples of living within our means. Countries under financial distress defer taking real action on austerity until much too late. For more than a year we've had a ringside seat watching Greece's government lurch towards the austerity measures required by foreign lenders before they deliver the next bailout installment to stop the country from going bankrupt. Amid riots and strikes, the government took months before legislating public salary cuts, tax hikes, raising the retirement age for government-funded pensions, cutting the minimum wage, and cutting government-funded pensions.

Companies do the same thing and some even get bailed out because they are "too big to fail". Chrysler and General Motors got government help to keep them afloat.

Unlike them, you are the perfect size to fail. Unless you're being sponsored by someone or still live in your parents' basement – you're going to participate 100 per cent in your own failure. You can't pass the blame or expense to someone or something else. This is your financial situation, your Pie, and only you own it.

Unlike a sovereign country, you cannot print money to make up for past policy mistakes.

If you borrow today you're effectively turning today's choice into tomorrow's debt obligation. You're reducing your choice for the future. That means the credit card debt you racked up when you over-indulged in retail therapy is now a pesky minimum monthly payment.

That changes your Pie because there's another slice gone – like the slices that go to taxes, housing, and transportation before you can even think about your own more personal and meaningful consumption.

Something else to keep in mind is that the future slice of Pie you're forfeiting will be larger than the piece of Pie you're borrowing to create the debt. It's called interest and it increases the amount you have to pay back.

One of my clients had a saying, "Borrow at a dollar and pay it back at two dollars." Debt can have severe consequences on your future Pie if you let it get out of control.

If you really want a reality check, look at all the interest you pay on all of your consumer debt: your car loan, line of credit and especially your mortgage. The mortgage payment structure is quite scary. Over the life of the amortization period of conventional mortgages, depending on interest rates, a significant portion of all your payments go towards interest.

Interest costs eat up your Pie – a whole lot more than a chain-smoking prisoner of war.

I've always wondered about the term "disposable income". It almost seems to suggest something of less value – like disposable diapers. Certainly it's transitory.

Remember, the amount left after servicing debts and paying for essentials is what you truly live on. When the cost of paying down your debt gets high enough, you may not feel like you have enough money to survive, let alone enough to enjoy life.

If what you have left of your Pie seems to amount to less than a hill of beans, remember that's your hill, and those are your beans.

After all, this is your Pie.

Comparing it to other Pies or to some ridiculous concept of perfection will only make you crazy. It sure won't do you any good.

Value who you are.

There's a slogan that should be posted on every bank and government building:

Live within your means.

Traps and Tricks

Don't drink the Kool-Aid

You see it as soon as you turn on your TV, open a newspaper, or hit the Internet. Everywhere you look you're bombarded by ads designed to get you to part with your cash for whatever product they're pushing.

You may groan when you see the ad, but consider that corporations part with billions every year to convince you to feed their bottom lines. Advertising agencies employ writers, graphics artists, actors, film directors and psychologists amongst others, to engineer ads. It's a multi-billion dollar business all about orchestrating how you spend your money.

Proctor & Gamble spent $4.18 billion in the United States in 2009 to convince you to buy Gillette, Olay, Cover Girl, Pantene and Tide.

Verizon Communications provides wireless service to millions of Americans, but in 2009 they still spent more than $3 billion on ads. Their biggest competitor, AT&T, didn't take that lying down. They spent $2.8 billion that year.

General Motors is the biggest auto maker in the U.S. They spent $2.2 billion on advertising in 2009.

The biggest pharmaceutical corporation in the world is Pfizer and they plan to keep that title. In 2009 they spent $2.1 billion to advertise their biggest money-makers including Lipitor and Viagra. Johnson & Johnson manufactures and markets pharmaceutical, health-care, and consumer items like Neutrogena, Tylenol and Aveeno. In 2009 they spent $2.06 billion to advertise their products.

Walt Disney Company may own the happiest places on earth, but the corporation spent $2 billion to convince you to vacation with them, watch their movies and videos, and keep your TV channel tuned to ESPN and ABC – which they also own.

Those are just the top advertisers in the U.S. for 2009, a year when advertising spending was down an estimated 35 per cent because of the recession.

We like to think of ourselves as reasonably sophisticated, or at least not completely gullible. But clearly advertising does what it's supposed to do – convince us to buy products. If it didn't work, don't you think executives would be using those billions to invest in new facilities or bigger bonuses for themselves?

Nobody is completely immune to advertising. When we don't consider how ads are dictating our spending, it's like we drank the Kool-Aid. We're buying what corporations are telling us we need.

I'm not talking about things we have to buy on a regular basis to maintain normal life functions. So this doesn't mean you're going to agonize over buying toilet paper.

The kinds of purchases I'm talking about are those described by any of the following phrases:

1. Something that's expensive to you
2. Something you already own at least one of
3. Something you feel pressured to buy
4. Something you don't really need

If you drank the Kool-Aid, and you're hypnotized by an ad, it may be too late to stop the momentum of the buying process.

However, here are some suggestions to change the way you look at a specific purchase. I call these **state-changers** or **a slap upside the head.**

Trap – stuff you already own

There's a famous George Carlin bit about stuff. He said, "*A house is just a pile of stuff with a cover on it.*"

We are a consumer society. We shop. Big and small things, houses, vehicles, clothes, technology, stuff for our kids. Whether we're ordering online or hitting the mall, we buy things. And keep them. Look around your house. Is it cluttered? Do you regularly use the stuff that gets in your way?

Do the possessions you have make you happy? Or does the clutter stress you out? There's a reason self-storage is a growth industry. When we get too much stuff to fit in our homes, we park the car in the driveway and fill the garage. When that's full too, we rent a storage unit and pay money each month to store items we obviously don't use. If we used them, we wouldn't put them in storage.

UCLA's Centre on Everyday Lives of Families studies contemporary society from an anthropological approach. They detailed their findings in a book called *Life at Home in the Twenty-First Century: 32 Families Open Their Doors.*

One home they examined had 2,260 visible possessions in three rooms: a living room, and two bedrooms. That didn't take into account all the objects in drawers, boxes and cabinets that weren't visible.

Interviewing parents in these homes, they discovered that mothers were almost universally unhappy with the clutter of possessions. They get stressed even seeing all the stuff that spills from one room to the next.

So how come we buy all this stuff?

One reason might be guilt. Dual income families are the norm these days, but we still feel guilty that mom works for money and therefore isn't at home for the kids 24/7. So we do something to make us feel a bit less guilty – we buy our kids toys. We want to give them everything we lacked as children. Now 10-year-old kids have smart phones and all the tech toys that adults lust after.

I'm not saying kids should have only one toy, or that they should be living in a state of privation. But really, do girls need two of every doll? Are kids really that gung-ho about Disney ornaments? Does a child in t-ball need a $200 mitt?

The estimate is that for every infant brought into the household, possessions increase by 30 per cent. Diaper bags, changing tables and strollers account for a small proportion of that. The rest are items we buy because we choose to.

We are surrounded, engulfed, and sometimes drowning in stuff we've bought. Does it make you happy?

If not, why do you assume more stuff will do the trick?

When you're thinking of buying something else, try some self-interventions….

Ask yourself – would you want to buy this if it meant spending the last of your money that you have available?

Remember my story in Chapter 2 about the homeless girl who sold her radio? She traded one of her few enduring life comforts for immediate, short-term comfort. This doesn't make her choice, or any choice, wrong. However, it should get us to look beyond the short-term comfort or happiness of a purchase to see if there's a long-term benefit that outweighs the long-term consequences or cost.

Ask yourself – if you had to give up two or five things you already own to buy it would you?

At the very least you can make it a condition of purchase. Whenever you buy something new, you have to get rid of a certain number of things you bought before. It would begin the process of weeding out some of the clutter in your home, but it's kind of an expensive way to accomplish that.

Ask yourself if your self-worth is a function of what you buy plus the opinion of others?

If that's true, then how **you** feel later about what you buy **may be unpredictable** – and most certainly the opinion of others at any time is **unpredictable. That means your sense of self-worth is a crapshoot every day.**

Would you always cherish it?

If your house was on fire, would this be one of the items you'd try to carry out of the flames?

What need does this purchase satisfy and is that my true taste?

Remember we're talking about your Pie. You aren't what you buy – what you buy is an extension of who you are. We all know deep down when we have made a good purchase no matter how much or how little it cost.

I've always believed that if the ride isn't worth the fall, you don't take the ride. I know I've made a good purchase when I'm comfortable with its consequences or cost. Sometimes you have to invest in yourself – your true self.

Death by a thousand slices

It seems the new focus today is not on what something costs, but the cost of carrying the payments for it. All of these extra payments can add up to consume a significant slice of your Pie. Think of the expression "death by a thousand cuts." Every debt payment represents a slice or cut of your Pie, whether it's large or small. How much taste would your Pie have for you if an ever-increasing number of cuts seriously diminished your ability to do what you wanted?

When a sale is a sale

Everybody loves buying on sale. Not only do we get to take something new home with us, we feel smart because we got a deal. But a deal is only a deal if you need it or want it or have a use for it.

The thing is, everybody has stuff at home they'll never wear or use because it was on sale and who could resist? Just because it's on sale, doesn't mean it's a deal for you.

Trick – 3 D Spending

Back in my old tax planning days, when it came to setting up basic income tax strategies, it was popular to use the three "Ds". They were:

1. Defer
2. Divide
3. Deduct

Now I use these three Ds in a different way to give you some spending strategies that may help you make better decisions. The basic concepts are pretty simple:

Defer - put off buying the object of your desire for a set time. Think of it as a cooling off period to give you time to consider all aspects of the purchase.

Divide - is it possible to buy less of it? If so and it still meets your needs – consider it.

Deduct - is it possible to replace this purchase with something that costs less? If a cheaper option meets your need – consider it.

Let's see how you could use the three "Ds" when you're baking your Pie.

We've all bought things that made us wonder what the hell we were thinking once we got them home. It would make a lot more sense to have those sober second thoughts before we buy something. A lot of major investments have a legislated cooling-off period to give the investor a reasonable amount of time to reconsider.

All I'm suggesting here is that you give yourself a cooling-off period before you make the actual purchase. Give yourself time to determine if you're doing the right thing.

I'll give you an example from my own life. I was in the U.S. on a business trip and saw a lovely leather-bound writing pad. I thought it would be ideal for taking client notes, and I could also use it to work on this book. I knew I could afford it and I could use it but the price was pretty steep. Then I kept thinking how I'd feel if I lost it, as I do travel quite a bit for my job.

I decided not to buy it and took my own advice regarding deferral. A month later, I knew I still wanted it so I bought it online.

I shared my story with a friend and business colleague. He told me he once saw a beautiful briefcase in a Japanese airport. He instantly fell in love with this briefcase but for many reasons that seemed valid at the time, he didn't buy it.

He told me he still regrets not buying it. He's been in many situations where that briefcase would have been useful and wonders if he'll ever find a similar one in another store.

Divide

Do you need all of this or will some of it do? Maybe you don't really need to buy two of something. Is it possible to get less of something and still be happy?

You should also consider renting to see if you really want or need it. My Uncle Delton had a great expression, "If I don't use it every day – I rent it."

This type of wisdom came in handy in the 80s when he was a farmer in southern Ontario. Farmers had just gone through a time of great prosperity, but times were changing. A lot of them had expensive equipment sitting on their farms. They bought or financed it during the boom times and the stuff just sat there waiting for the seasons to change so it would be useful. My uncle had been smart enough to rent what he needed and return it when he was done. This meant he had a lot less debt and capital tied up in equipment he didn't use all the time.

This type of strategy also works in reverse. You shouldn't rent something you use every day. I know times can be tough but a lot of these rent-to-own companies charge a lot of the purchase price for items like household appliances and furniture. Sometimes it's better to do without and wait until you can afford to buy it, rather than pay someone a premium to have it now.

Deduct

Replace the purchase with something else. It seems simple, doesn't it? Before we start this section I want you to remember something. **I believe the ongoing cost of your ego is the most expensive thing you'll ever afford yourself in your life.**

If something of lesser cost looks as good and feels as good as a more expensive option, **who cares what you paid for it**? Contrary to popular belief, there's no prize for having all the best toys, technology and dishes if you're the only one who cares what you paid for them. Impressing others is a slippery slope. Buying something to impress is temporary, but the debts arising from the purchase can last a long time.

I remember having enough points to get myself into the first-class lounge at a New York airport on a business trip. I struck up a conversation with a native New Yorker. He was a businessman who worked in the financial district. He seemed very impressive to me and certainly looked the part of a successful New York stockbroker. I noticed his watch and complimented him on it. I thought it was a Rolex. He told me he bought it for $50 from a street vendor just outside his Wall Street office. He said he couldn't tell the difference between this knock-off watch and the real thing, so he decided to buy it and use the money he saved for more useful things.

It made no sense for him to pay $2,000 or more for something that tells time and looks good. For the $50 he spent, I was impressed and he was happy. Forget the media and advertising hype here.

He wasn't trying to hide the fact that he had paid $50 for a knock-off Rolex – in fact he was quite proud of it. Doing what makes you feel good and spending less for it is a recipe for happiness and true-tasting *Life, By The Pie*.

TRAP – You have to guard the mental needs hard drive in your head – don't let something you want become something you need.

We spend a lot of time, energy and money protecting our computer hard drives against viruses and hackers. But how much effort do we put into protecting our minds from media, advertising, peer pressure, and other external forces of influence? The answer is not much, and certainly not enough.

When a hacker or virus takes over your computer you lose control of it, and the hard drive can be compromised. Sometimes the damage is so great it renders the computer useless. Because this damage or loss of control is immediate and obvious it makes the computer owner respond quickly to try to undo or repair the damage.

When someone tries to control you by hacking into the needs hard drive in your head, you usually don't even notice. You assume a change in your opinion or behaviour is your choice. You don't consider the behaviour might have been dictated by someone or something external. You're allowing your mind to be hijacked by whatever external agency is defining how your needs will be met.

It seems that all great action heroes in the movies need a certain look to make them real tough guys. One common trait I noticed was that they all had great sunglasses. Even bad asses have to protect their eyes in style. These sunglasses were apparently so necessary that tough guys even wear them at night. Style trumps vision anytime – day or night.

I remember going to a big retail store seeking that special look in eyewear. I tried on a cheap version of the real thing that would've set me back about $250. I looked in the mirror and my first thought was, "Damn, I could use an automatic weapon and a toothpick for my mouth to finish this look."

If you want another example of an assault on your needs hard drive, think of how smoking has been portrayed over the years. Especially in the movies of the 40s and 50s, they made smoking look sexy. There are even some famous scenes in movies where lighting a cigarette and giving it to your love interest was portrayed as a unique and sexy style move.

These images of sexiness exist even though we know this product causes death and is highly addictive. It also costs a whole lot of money. There is nothing sexy about lung cancer but smoking still has a certain cache that causes many people to start smoking every day and prevents others from quitting.

Advertising for these products is highly regulated and the product is highly taxed. We know smoking is bad for us. We know a lot of bad things about this product, yet still some people choose to smoke. It's like someone else is driving you and you're just along for the ride.

Everybody wants something from you – your money, your time, your opinion. Everyone wants to engage you in some form of conversation or interaction. Businesses, charities, and even govern-ments dedicate big money and lots of personnel to find out how to get your personal information. Market research and polling are your opponents when it comes to guarding your needs hard drive.

In Judo, you learn to use an opponent's own momentum or weakness to your advantage. Everyone has a weakness. That weakness is revealed the more opponents interact. The more your opponent knows about you, how you move and how you think, the more s/he can use some form of leverage against you. In the same way, once an organization has gotten information about you by hook or by crook, they can use that information and your weaknesses as leverage against you. Once they've learned how to do that, they control your hard drive.

This is why you keep getting those phone calls asking you a few simple survey questions. The surveys are always supposed to be brief and a lot of us are basically nice, and we cooperate. I usually get these calls around supper time when I'm supposedly most likely to be home. It's a good thing that about that time of day I have the attention span of a goldfish. As politely as possible I disengage from the caller.

Things that really matter to you don't need a hard sell. They command all your attention effortlessly. When something resonates with you deeply over a long period of time, it is usually a good indication of what decision is the right one. Just like an old love in a relationship that you thought you was over and done with, you can't stop thinking about what or who you're missing. Your heart rules your head in many situations. As I have said before, something becomes a good buy if you know you will always cherish it.

Trap – You Deserve It
but "Deservin' ain't got nothin' to do with it"

I was watching an old Western where this real bad guy has just been shot by another guy he really ticked off. While lying on the saloon floor the bad guy says to the guy who just shot him: "I don't deserve this."

To which the shooter replied: "Deservin' ain't got nothin' to do with it."

Right before he got shot, this real bad guy beat up, maimed, or killed a lot of people – including people the shooter cared about. In my estimation, the bad guy got exactly what he deserved.

Not surprisingly, he didn't see it that way as he lay bleeding out on the bar room floor. How many times have you thought you deserved to buy something you wanted? Because you're a good person, or you've done without in the past, you had a rough day at work, or you had a fight with your kids, or maybe a commercial really caught your eye.

There's a reason one brand of hair products has used the slogan, "because I'm worth it," for years. At some point we all figure we deserve more.

Maybe your assessment about "deservin" is about as accurate as a dying cowboy.

We all know someone with spending problems who has perfectly good reasons for his bad behaviour. Sometimes he buys himself something as a reward; sometimes she buys something as a comfort when she's feeling down. Bottom line, this kind of retail therapy has a sense of "deservin" at its core.

In the 21st century, it seems like everyone is special. Nothing is your fault as long as you can find a reason for your bad behaviour. I've seen people bring themselves to financial ruin because they latched on to an excuse for giving themselves short-term gratification regardless of the long-term harm they caused themselves.

Just like the smoking example, the comfort of that next cigarette pales in comparison to the long-term damage that comes from the habit.

I'm not sure anyone deserves anything. If I hit a bad golf shot it can go in the woods and be lost, or it can carom off a tree and bounce back on the fairway. In either case, the ball goes where it goes and it has no concept of what I deserve.

Certainly there are things that are earned, or won or given, but I think those are different issues than what we're talking about here. Let me be clear. I'm talking about things you're not sure you should buy because they're expensive, or you can't afford them. Or you're not sure you really need them. But you want them.

Don't ever let the words "because I deserve it" creep into the reasoning behind a purchase.

Avoid the trap – remember the words spoken to the dying cowboy.

"Deservin' ain't got nothin' to do with it."

Ultimate Trick - The Daily Dish
& the power of focus

It's hard to make changes in your life when you don't know where to start or what to focus on.

If you don't know where your money is really going on a regular basis, it's nearly impossible to recognize the areas and expenses that can be modified and/or eliminated to make your life better.

The *Daily Dish* , which you can activate at no charge (please see the **Activate Your Free Life, By The Pie Account** section at the end of this book), enables you to list your daily expenses, and then summarizes them in an easy-to-read format. These daily totals can be summarized into weeks, months and (if necessary) years, so you can really see what you spend your money on.

From the summaries, you and you alone can decide what changes you want to make to your behaviour to make your life's Pie taste good to you...

It would be great to tell you that the process of the *Daily Dish* is going to solve all your problems, but you know that's not true. Life has many challenges and every day will be different. Your expenses can be predictable to some extent – but life never is.

Here are some things I want you to remember as you use this process:

1. Sometimes we get good breaks we don't deserve. It might be an unexpected windfall or your expenses will be low for a little while.
2. Sometimes you get bad breaks you don't deserve. Stuff happens – and that's the polite term for it. We all have unexpected expenses and emergencies we have to deal with.
3. Sometimes you're going to have long stretches of time where your earnings and/or expenses are going really well – which means you're going to have to learn how to deal with success.
4. Sometimes you'll have long stretches of time where there are very few good days and you're going to have to learn to deal with that too.

I say all this so you understand that nobody's perfect and that good and bad things happen to everybody. It's up to you to keep moving toward your goals.

If you've ever been on a diet, you probably kept a journal where you logged what you ate and drank every day. It gives you the power to look back and figure out when you over-indulged and why. It also teaches you portion control.

Think of the *Daily Dish* as an exercise in financial portion control that will also let you look back and figure out your spending triggers.

Some time ago, I went through a routine audit of my finances by those wonderful people in the Canadian government called the Canada Revenue Agency. When they were done with me, the one big change I knew I had to make was to start keeping a log of my travel expenses. Even though it seemed I was driving a lot for business, I couldn't prove it because I hadn't kept a written record.

I thought that keeping a log would be difficult, but I knew that I never wanted to be caught lacking that information again. I started to record my travel expenses every business day. It was so easy. The logbook is right beside me in the car and I make an entry in the morning before I start the car. Once I started recording everything, I was blown away by how much travelling I was doing for business.

Your *Daily Dish* is always there for you on your mobile device. Record your expenses as you make your purchases.

Remember: **If something is worth spending money on it is worth recording.**

I knew a guy who was taking care of his elderly aunt some years back. He was in his 50s and single and she was in her 90s living in a nursing home. He was the joint account holder on all her bank accounts and used the money to take care of all her expenses. He visited her regularly and was quite close to her. Everyone knew that he genuinely cared for her and always used the money from her accounts for her benefit.

As time went on, she started to give him money because she knew she was in her final years and got joy out of helping him while she was still alive. She also felt a lot closer to him than to anyone else in her family. Some in his family were jealous of those gifts but apparently not jealous enough to make the effort to visit the aunt regularly.

He used this money to travel and for home improvements. Over the years these gifts added up to a substantial amount of money.

When his aunt died things started to get nasty. One of the executors of the estate questioned the nature and size of those financial gifts. Even though it was generally accepted that he had done everything above board and according to his aunt's wishes, **he could not prove it because he never kept a record.**

The courts take a very dim view of anyone who has access to an elderly person's assets who appears to be using them for personal benefit. He was ordered to pay the estate about $60,000.

This is why the *Daily Dish* is so important – it helps you record all your expenses, even the little ones. Once something is recorded, it's a lot tougher to ignore. If you're going to make a change in your life you have to start with telling yourself the truth. Most of the time, the truth doesn't seem as bad as you thought it would be. No matter what, like everything in life, you learn to handle it.

The nice thing about the *Daily Dish* is that there's a new Dish every day. That means you have a fresh chance every morning to make a better tasting Pie. The past doesn't have to determine your future. You can make every day the best it can be.

There's a lot to be said about the benefits of failure. It's not all bad if you choose to learn from your mistakes. Making necessary changes and moving on without beating yourself up about not being perfect will be one of the key ingredients to change.

Make it fun to do your *Daily Dish*. Don't make it a test of your self-worth. Make it a game – how little money can I spend today and still make my life's Pie taste good?

Who you are is not defined necessarily by the Pie you have right now. Who you are can be defined by the daily decisions you make that will give you the best future Pie. You're not alone if you start to worry your Pie isn't good enough. The outside world has hypnotized many people to believe that no matter what they do, it just won't be good enough. We screw up because we're human. But because we're human, we can learn from our mistakes.

Without fear there's no courage. Only you can know how hard or perhaps easy changing will be.

Instead of focusing on the past, or the details involved with the changes you want to make, focus on the joy of living a life that's fully engaged. You're doing something every day that's going to make your life better. It's part of our human nature to want to learn and grow. The regular focus the *Daily Dish* provides will help you learn and grow, and can bring you some personal satisfactions along the way.

I really believe that we are much more than our current bank balance, the house we live in, the friends we have, and any trappings of success and status we have. I think we all have within us the capacity to find joy in just being who we are.

In my 20s I threw javelin with a pretty impressive group of guys. Two of the men I threw with actually went on to compete in the Olympics. The group was centered at the University of Toronto and on a regular basis we competed with another group of equally impressive guys from the Ottawa area.

Whenever we went to track meets, it always seemed that most of the guys from those two groups were in the top eight. Being a top eight, meant you made the finals where you were allowed three more throws. Making the finals was a big deal.

Usually I made the finals even if it was seventh or eighth. There was a guy, I'll just call him Bob, who rarely made the finals in those early years. Bob was from Ottawa and my coach used to make fun of him saying he had a "rubber arm."

One thing I really liked about him was that he loved throwing javelin and learning all he could about the sport and the people in it. Bob loved the process of learning and throwing – he was a javelin junkie.

Bob refused to accept the idea that you're only as good as how far you can throw. He got better every year. Then one year he decided to really learn the sport so he moved to Finland. Finland is the Mecca of javelin throwing. It's like the Holy Land to throwers. When Bob came back from Finland he not only threw farther, but he could tell all his dirty jokes in Finnish. This guy with the "rubber arm" kicked our butts when he came back to Canada.

The unique thing about Bob was that he was the same guy whether he came first or last in a competition. Most of the throwers I've been friends with over the years are exactly like that. We all love the process of throwing spears and the people involved in our sport.

In later years Bob had an injury that ended his career, but he always seemed at peace with himself because he'd done something he loved and did it to the best of his ability.

I've met many people who retire from sports or work who aren't satisfied with what they accomplished. They realize when it's too late that there were things they could have done better, and they seem to live in regret.

I don't want that for you.

Doing the *Daily Dish* process and doing the best you can every day will reduce your risk of regret in the future. Hopefully you'll learn to enjoy life more as well.

Retraining yourself to live by your own taste

I think it's safe to say we have all purchased things in the past that we didn't really need or want and those things didn't bring us joy.

I want to move on to the basic philosophy of the *Daily Dish*. Think of it as a daily training program that will help you discover what you need on a daily basis to make you happy and productive. Finding your own true taste is going to be your personal journey of discovery. You alone will decide what is necessary for you on a daily basis. By recording each purchase every day, you'll see the content and consequences of your choices. Then you can decide within yourself whether you want to make a change.

This means instead of spending a certain percentage of your income – just because you can – on whatever you want to buy, I'll ask you to focus on what consistent expenditures are really necessary to make your life work and make your Pie taste good to you.

Giving up what you might want in the moment for things you truly need for the long-term is a recipe for success. When you get the things you truly want or need by saving or investing, you'll also experience a sense of personal satisfaction that only you can give yourself.

Being true to your own taste is a foreign concept to most of us because we've been told for most of our lives what's good for us. Living life according to your own taste means you seek outside approval less and rely on your own approval more.

If learning how to run your own brain isn't enough motivation for you, I'll give you a few more reasons before we get into the details of the Daily Dish program.

I've heard it said that a lot of people major in minor things. If you look at the spending decisions you make day in and day out, all the mistakes you make add up to be major outlays of your resources. Frittering away your money on a regular basis means that you're likely missing out on things of major significance that you could have added to your life had you spent your money better.

Remember my golden rule:
He Who Has The Gold Makes The Rules.

Saving money and amassing cash resources will make you more significant to yourself and to others. If you have any doubt about this – ask someone who constantly borrows money to get by, just how significant he feels on a regular basis.

I'll tell you a couple of stories. These stories occurred about the same time in my life. One showed me the kind of significance money could buy and the other showed me the kind of significance I didn't want to buy.

One of my first jobs was selling real estate in North Toronto. I was in my early 20s and real estate prices at the time were a far cry from what they are today. You could get a good home in Toronto then for under $200,000. That's why some people call them the good old days.

One summer day, a gentleman visited our real estate office and asked for the agent in charge. Usually the duty agent gets first crack at a walk-in client, but the duty agent that day didn't want to deal with an old guy who was wearing old clothes and smelled of fish. The guy was also carrying a greasy paper bag with him that seemed to have his lunch inside.

Finally, one of the older agents took the man into his office and started showing him pictures of homes in the area. After a while they decided on a few interesting properties and went out in the agent's car to have a look.

When they came back, we noticed our agent now smelled of fish just like his client, but they seemed to be getting along and headed into his office. We all knew from our razor sharp perception of wealth that our fellow agent was wasting his time.

As the story came out, the old guy decided he liked one of the homes he saw. When the agent asked him how he'd like to pay for it, the old guy said, "Why don't we use this?" Then he emptied the contents of his greasy paper bag onto the agent's desk and asked him to start counting.

The man had $80,000 cash in the bag and was able to buy the home without any problem. Our agent friend made a nice commission for three hours of work and we all got a lesson in perception.

Significance comes in many forms. As they say in my business, "Money talks and BS walks". True significance doesn't come from throwing money away on trivia – it comes from having the resources to get what you really want.

I believe there's a certain level of significance we can all attain by saving our money and spending it more wisely when the opportunity arises. However, there are certain levels of significance you may choose not to buy.

As I mentioned earlier, I was this young stud in Toronto selling real estate in the north part of the city. Through my travels I met this very attractive young lady. When I got the chance to get to know her, I found myself quite smitten with her.

I thought that doing something I really loved made me significant. I thought being confident that one day I'd be successful would be enough to attract someone into my life. There was a lesson to be learned here.

As I got to know this young lady better and better I learned that her previous relationship was with the son of a very wealthy Toronto family. She really seemed to miss this guy and one day I got up the courage to ask her why. She told me that she really missed the shopping trips to New York he took her on. He would even give her money to spend on these trips.

I figured that with my current income, it would take me about five years to have enough money in a greasy paper bag to give her one week's worth of what this other guy used to give her on a regular basis. I knew I was out of my league and moved on.

I don't miss her.

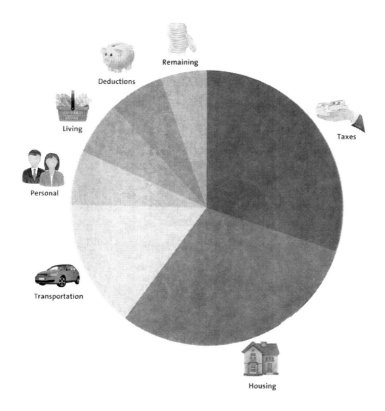

Killer Kool-Aid Kombos

Now that we have a basic understanding of the external forces likely to attack our needs hard drive, let's examine what happens when one purchase seems to meet two or more needs.

Remember, the more needs that seem to be satisfied with a purchase, the more powerful the influence upon you.

Killer Kombo #1 -
Crust (security) and Sugar (love, connection)

Is there anything parents wouldn't do to protect their child?

Watch any ad for home security systems. Usually it starts with the threat of a bad guy getting inside the home. That's a basic threat to security. The bad guy is in the house when the alarm goes off and the security system scares the bad guy away.

Afterwards, the kids are safe, and mom and dad are happy.

Make no mistake, these types of systems are necessary and useful, but to make you take action the ads first scare the crap out of you and then make it all better by selling you on their product.

Remember, it's not what they're selling you – it's **how** they're selling you on a product or service that's important here. You must guard against making decisions based on external manipulation. You need to ask yourself what buttons an advertiser is pushing. Then you need to figure out your needs and base your shopping decision on your reality, not what a corporation is telling you your needs are.

Killer Kombo #2 -
Crust (comfort) + Filling (variety, fun) + Savoury/Spice (Significance) + Sugar (Connection, Love)

With alcohol you hit the needs jackpot. It's not hard to figure out why alcohol addiction is one of the worst problems facing our society today. Think about it. You have a drink and you know absolutely that after a few more you're going to be in a different state. You might feel more confident, sexier, powerful, or simply more social. Alcohol brings a state change that is predictable and one that many of us find at least temporarily desirable. Lots of comfort/crust there.

Look at the ads for any alcohol product. You'll see a lot of people having a really good time (filling). They're all really attractive and hip (Spice). And they seem to be friends who really enjoy each other's company (Sugar).

Now I love getting out and having drinks and fun with friends as much as the next person. However, I think it makes sense to understand that it's not just the taste of alcohol that makes it so addictive. Any time the consumption of one product can fill so many needs, there's going to be a strong pull to consume.

Gambling has much the same allure as alcohol. When you gamble it takes you to another world. A world you perceive to be better than your daily work-a-day reality. There's a comfort in that. Traditional casino or race track gambling also gets you out of the house so there's some variety and fun to that as well. If you win you feel special. Lucky. Significant.

Do you think casinos give out player cards because they want to recycle plastic? Being a regular at a casino gives some people significance and a sense of belonging.

I don't think I need to go on much about this. The old saying "everything in moderation" is what I advocate. I gamble and I drink but I keep it under control because I've seen the devastation when people can't control their behaviour when it comes to drinking and/or gambling.

Killer Kombo #3 -
Crust (comfort) + Filling (variety, fun) + Savoury/Spice (Significance) + Sugar (Connection, Love)

The business of sport is a multibillion dollar industry all over the world because it satisfies a wide spectrum of basic needs for all different cultures. In fact, all the ingredients of your life's Pie can be experienced at an event with your favorite team – at a premium price of course.

Are you a fan of hockey? Let's take a look at a team that has recently been valued at $1 billion even though it hasn't won a championship since 1967 – the Toronto Maple Leafs.

They may not win, but being a Leaf fan fulfills a wide spectrum of needs.

Comfort, security (crust)

The Leafs are steeped in hockey tradition that goes back to the early 1900s. Their history is well-documented and revered. After all, the team is one of the Original Six teams in the National Hockey League. This team has endured through the worst of times and has long been a symbol of hope for many. Everyone can remember watching or listening to broadcasts of Leafs games surrounded by the comfort and security of family and friends.

The Leaf organization respects the past by honoring former players in ceremonies at games. They also host old-timers events so the public can see their childhood heroes.

Variety, adventure (filling)

Going to games is fun. You never know the outcome of any game until the final buzzer. Sport is unpredictable by nature and sometimes you see something in a hockey game that you've never seen before in your life. I know from first-hand experience that the Leafs are both capable of beating anyone and losing to anyone on any given night. It's the agony and the ecstasy of cheering for a team that makes life an adventure, I think.

Significance (spice)

You want to be somebody special? How about platinum seats to see your team? Better yet – look at the "in" crowd that watches games from private boxes. Not everyone can get into those hallowed areas because there's tight security to keep a distance between the privileged and special separate from common fans in the so-called cheap seats.

Love connection (sugar)

One of the Leafs' slogans is "the passion that unites us all". It's something all Leaf fans truly believe. I know that for certain because I've been a Leaf fan all my life. Whenever they start to win, certain friends will call me out of nowhere to talk about "our" Leafs.

I understand human needs and I know sports, but I still feel pretty special whenever I go to a game. I confess that I'm a fan, always have been and always will be, and I'm hoping they win another Stanley Cup some time before I die.

Killer Kombo #4 -
Crust (comfort) + Filling (variety, fun) + Savoury/Spice (Significance) + Sugar (Connection, Love)

We all need some form of transportation. The cost of a car is the second most expensive asset most of us will own. Your home will probably be the most expensive. The car industry is another multi-billion dollar industry that has customers worldwide. This is a high stakes game in which car companies make sure they understand what makes people pay a premium for personal transportation. They know that a car can be so much more to us than simply transportation.

Variety, adventure (Filling)

The open road. The wind in your hair. Movement. Everybody wants to get out and have fun. You don't have to explain what a car means to a teenager who just got his license. It means freedom. It means excitement. It means moving away from the comfort and boredom of home to the variety of the open road. This is not the car in which his parents drove him to soccer practice.

Significance (Spice)

Having the right car could mean everything to you.

I drive a car that supports an image I portray for my job. I have to play the game like everyone else does to some extent. Cars meet a certain status or they can reflect some aspect of your personality.

A hot muscle car could mean you are manly and adventurous. A great truck could mean you are manly and hard-working. (I always love the truck ads with the guy with the deep manly voice.)

Look at any ad for a new automobile. It's clear the advertisers know their target audience and push every button they can to entice them to buy the advertised vehicle.

Connection, love (Sugar)

There is nothing good parents won't do to protect their children. Only vehicles with great safety records and/or lots of room are going to be desirable when choosing the family car.

Comfort, security (Crust)

Everyone needs a reliable vehicle. Someone who has to contend with a severe winter isn't going to feel good driving an expensive Italian sports car in a snow storm. We all want cars that will last and not cost a lot to maintain and operate.

When it comes to vehicles, I think it's important to look at how much household income is spent on transportation.

When I was in my 20s, I knew guys who were spending more than 50 per cent of their take-home pay on sports cars. They drank the Kool-Aid every day and even in their dreams. They were car-poor. It's important to make sure the cost of your vehicle is reasonable – a price you can afford without pulling cash required to provide for other needs.

Summary: Knowing who you are and who you are not

Awareness of how your needs factor in any purchase is one thing; what you choose to do about it is quite a different matter. You have every right to freely choose what you want to buy, so long as you're aware of the cost or consequences.

This is where the philosophy of *Life, By The Pie*™ may be different from any other book you read on financial/cash management. I'm not trying to make you perfect, or program you to behave like a robot. I want you to make decisions understanding why you made those choices and the consequences of them.

I'll give you two examples that may help make my point.

A few years ago I had a discussion with a friend about a guy he'd met. It seems this fellow was super disciplined. He got up at 5 a.m. to beat the traffic into work, packed his lunch to save money, knew where he spent every dime, and had seven per cent body fat, a perfect wife and 2.5 kids (okay-he had two kids). At the end of describing him, my buddy exclaimed, "What a boring life!" I think both of us thought someday this man was going to crack under the pressure of being so perfect.

The other example comes from more recent times. I saw a news report about a guy on trial for arson. It seemed he felt he had to burn down his house to save himself from financial ruin.

Until this point in his life, everything seemed perfect. He was a local celebrity and a man many admired. The news report showed how he'd gone on a mountaineering expedition to launch a new charity. Old news clips showed him being interviewed live while climbing. The local news station really loved him. Later, after the climb was completed, local authorities determined his charity was bogus and shut it down.

He was that guy all men supposedly want to be and all women supposedly want. He had great hair and the media loved him – what else mattered?

One problem – he just wasn't that guy.

At the arson trial it all began to unravel. A life of pretense and media spin caught up to him. In court it was revealed he didn't have all the money he said he had. He burned his house down because he was in real financial trouble.

He just wasn't that guy.

For someone whose whole life was based on an image and good first impressions, to be revealed for what he really was devastated him.

He committed suicide right after the verdict was read.

It is important you don't try to be perfect. It's also important that you don't try to be something you're not.

Knowing every day is a new day and it's okay to make mistakes is what life is all about. The *Life, By The Pie*™ philosophy makes it easier for you to live with yourself and be happy with what you have.

Don't beat yourself up about mistakes – use the program to learn why you spend money the way you do and decide what you want to do about it. The program is just a tool and you control it.

As time goes on you will learn more about yourself. When you're ready and when you really want to, you will do the things you know are necessary to make your life better and live by your true taste.

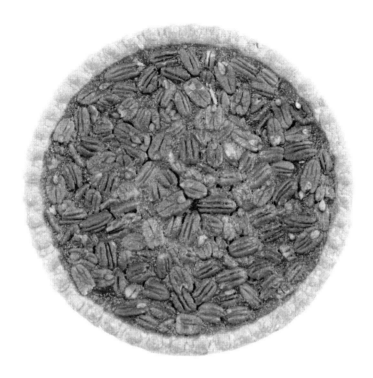

Let's Start Baking

Now that we've talked about why we spend our money and the consequences of those decisions, I think it's very important that the rest of this book is dedicated to the actual baking of different Pies. There are three situations I want to cover.

1. The Pies you make for yourself
2. The Pies you help others to make
3. The future Pies you make

The Pies You Make For Yourself

The *Life, By The Pie*™ program has many ways to improve the way your life "tastes" by helping you understand yourself. I want you to enroll in the University of You. Give yourself at least 90 days to make your Pie over and over again, each time using what you've learned about yourself by recording your daily spending in the *Daily Dish* module. With each new view of your overall Pie, you can decide what changes you want to make in your life and what direction you want your life to take.

Understand something here. I see money as a servant to our desires. With the proper discipline, I believe that our money lives for us – we do not live for our money. That means it is okay to want and buy something as long as it does not put other more bona fide needs at risk.

When you start your first Pie there will be many regular or time-related expenses that you know you have. These are expenses like mortgage payments, all loan/lease/rent payments, and all monthly payments for utilities and Internet related expenses. Your cable and cell phone bills would also go here.

After you've put in all the expenses you know you have to pay, it will be interesting for you to see how much cash is really left in your Pie at this point. Look at what's left before you start to consider the day-to-day, out-of-pocket expenses you incur.

If you know roughly what you spend on the expense categories that are not regular, then by all means put them in. However for most of us the next step in the process is to start using the *Daily Dish* module on a regular basis. You can make this as "regular" as you want. The purpose of the *Daily Dish* module is to identify the details of your spending over time.

You may not realize how much you spend on something until you see the results from a week or a month of the *Daily Dish*. You can "do the dish" until you have a handle on your spending and then record your results in the *Life, By The Pie*™ program to give your calculations more detail, and therefore more accuracy.

You may also decide to use the *Daily Dish* module when you want to monitor expenses for significant events and/or time periods. Examples of this would be:

1. Christmas season spending
2. Vacation spending
3. Business trip spending

"Doing the dish" helps you in your studies at the University of You. After observing yourself on a regular basis, you and you alone decide if you are getting a passing grade in finances. Once you understand the significance that small daily changes can make in your life, you start to develop your personal integrity muscle more and more. You learn the satisfaction of making and keeping promises to yourself.

An example of this is a trip I took to Chicago just before Christmas of 2012. I had a budget for the trip and a limit or guidance for Christmas shopping. The flight and hotel were set amounts that I knew before I went. The only variables were food, entertainment, and of course, the shopping.

My plans are always fluid when I'm in a new city. If there's something special to do, and I may not be back for a long time, I will do it. In this case a classic Broadway show was playing nearby. The cost of tickets made other expenditures, like truly fine dining and a Bull's game, go by the wayside. Going to that show was very special to both my wife and me. It was worth the price we paid.

On this particular trip, my money seemed to go farther when I was buying gifts for friends and family. I tried to buy items that came with free samples or gifts that I could use as stocking stuffers. Christmas is a great time to use this strategy. I'm not a shopping expert, but I'm a pretty good expert when it comes to me. I'm enrolled in the University of Me and I'm learning all the time. I always think I'm passing the course if I feel satisfied with what I've spent money on and how much I've spent.

I had the money to do a lot more but I decided to keep to a certain limit on the trip. On my way home I had no regrets about what I'd spent on the trip or on the Christmas shopping I had done. That means the taste of my Pie and the size of my slices are consistent with my life's true taste.

Since this is my Pie, that's all that matters.

Enroll yourself into the University of You, start making Pies, and "do the dish".

Start enjoying life on your own terms.

The Pies you help others to make

When you start making Pies you really like on a regular basis, you may want to help someone else that you care about make better Pies for him/herself .Everyone else's life seems so easy to change – from a distance. I'm amazed how smart and wise some people on daytime TV are when it comes to dishing out advice on how everyone should live their lives. I think we all know that effecting real change in someone else takes a lot more than sage sound bites.

If we're going to really try to help someone with their spending, we have to help them bake their own Pies. That means helping them understand the consequences of their financial choices by seeing the results for themselves. Someone making bad Pies is doing the best s/he can in their own way. To bring about real change you have to take all the negative emotions of judgment and blame out of the exercise and let the Pie speak for itself.

The best way to help is to encourage them to enroll in their own University of You. They have to understand the size of their slices. Let it all sink in. Help them to own their own Pies. Encourage them to "do the dish" for 30 days to better understand where their money is going, and where in their budget they can reasonably make changes. It also allows people to identify the problems without getting paralyzed by emotions.

Remember, I'm the guy who believes in gravity and math. Gravity is pretty easy to understand. Math feels like the latest dying language – on its way to the same linguistic graveyard as Latin. I am amazed by how many people I encounter every day that seem to have little or no understanding of basic math. If not understanding math is the new normal, then *Life, By The Pie™* may be the tool of choice to help people retain control of their finances. It's a program designed for modern times with a timeless symbol – the Pie. A symbol of consumption everyone can relate to.

Everyone understands slices or portions. The Pie and Dish programs can be used with any mobile device or computer. If you're trying to help someone, you have to put in their hands the power to effect change in themselves. Few people in the civilized world do not have access to modern technology. Powerful change can take place if you're using the tools and/or toys you use every day to solve your financial problems.

I helped a couple of my clients use the program to effect change in their daughter.

Life, By The Pie Example - Grandma's Old Car

A couple I worked with for many years – I will call them Bill and Barbara – had a daughter named Amy who was 25 and living away from home for the first time.

I thought Amy was a fine young woman, but she was having a lot of trouble with money and needed to ask her parents for help from time to time. Every time she went for help, it caused a lot of heat on both sides.

Her parents thought they had somehow failed because their daughter couldn't make ends meet at the ripe old age of 25. She hated asking for money because it usually came with an historical retrospective about how things were when her parents were 25.

Amy lived in a town in her own apartment. Grandma had given Amy her old car which was about 15 years old and in running condition – barely. Amy used this car to drive to her first job working at a pharmacy in the next city. This drive was about an hour each way and took up a lot of her time. She also had some student debt to pay, and was going to night school twice a week.

Amy was a hard-working girl and Bill and Barbara were good parents. They had a problem that was steeped in so much emotion that it paralyzed them all.

Barbara remembered when Amy was still living at home and used to spend all the money she made at her part-time job on clothes. Barbara was certain that it was Amy's love for clothes that was causing all her money problems.

Bill hated seeing everyone so upset. The arguments between his wife and Amy got loud and intense. They really knew how to push each other's buttons. All Bill could relate to was his own upbringing – he'd been out on his own at 21. He never had a lot of money as a young man and thinks a lot of young people today are spoiled.

Amy was a busy girl. Math was not her strong suit. She worked long hours, commuted two hours a day and got home at 9 p.m. twice a week when she went to night school. She had no idea where her money was going and she had no perspective on what things should cost. She told me she only spent money on things she really needed. She just couldn't figure out why she was so broke all the time.

I asked Bill and Barb to help Amy make a Pie and review all the slices with me. Here's a summary of what it looked like:

Amy was making about $30,000 year at her pharmacy job. Out of that she had to pay approximately $6,000 a year in taxes. Of the remaining $24,000 per year she had left she paid about $12,000 in rent for her apartment. I had no comment so far as I had no idea what market rents were for where she lived, but I knew that for Amy, it was a lot to spend for a place to live.

Then we got to the piece of the Pie that really caught my attention – transportation. It turned out it was costing Amy $150 a week to drive Grandma's old car. Add about $3,000 for insurance because of all the driving she did and her youth. That meant that of out of the $12,000 that remained after she paid her rent, about $10,000 a year was spent on driving Grandma's old car.

That means that Amy had roughly $2000 a year to spend on food, clothes and student debt.

Suddenly math took over and emotions hit the sidelines. Now there were real issues that we could discuss and analyze. Those issues were:

1. the cost of Grandma's old car
2. the cost of commuting to a job so far away
3. the cost of an apartment

Amy had no life experience that would have helped her realize she was spending too much on something. She never had any discussions about what she could afford and/or what things should cost. She also felt that she would be seen as ungrateful if she complained about the cost of running Grandma's car, but it was a gas guzzling boat that also cost a lot of money to repair. She liked living close to family and friends but knew the commuting was not only costly, but could get quite dangerous in the winter, especially in Grandma's car.

Everyone was doing the best they could, especially Amy, but the math was working against her. She thought it was the car that was causing all the trouble, however no one had ever sat down with her and showed her how big a slice the car took of her Pie.

Amy needed help making a Pie without the outside ingredients of blame and guilt. After a few months, Amy got a job closer to home and started taking the bus. Grandma's old car was donated to the Salvation Army.

People get stuck

Whenever you try to help someone, understand that sometimes people just get stuck in a rut. They do the same thing over and over again, but are too caught up in the problem to see solutions.

When I was about 20 years of age and still in university, I was driving a tanker truck on Christmas break for a local service firm. I was trying to get a few days of work in before Christmas so that I'd have enough money to buy presents for everyone. On my last day of driving, it started to snow in the morning and snowed all day. By the time I was on my last call, there was a lot of snow on the ground and I got stuck in a customer's driveway.

The truck was a powerful one with four rear wheels altogether in the rear end. The two rear wheels on my passenger side were stuck in a soft shoulder and I tried rocking the truck to get out of the rut I was in. I must've tried this rocking strategy for about half an hour until finally, and much to my relief, I finally got myself out. I was driving home feeling pretty good about myself and my truck driving skills, when there was a slight jolt followed by the appearance of a tire rolling down the highway past me on the passenger side of the truck.

This tire looked strangely familiar. I was sure I'd seen it before, but it wasn't until the truck jolted again and listed badly towards the passenger side that I realized the tire was mine. As it turned out, my efforts to get myself out of the rut had weakened the bolts that kept the wheels attached to the truck, and they gave up the ghost on my ride home.

I called my boss. He was very angry with me and called a tow truck driver. I was upset. I felt I had done something wrong but wasn't sure what it was. It was just before Christmas and I needed the money from this job very badly.

When the tow truck driver appeared, he calmly did all that was necessary to get the wheels back on the truck and send me on my way. While he was doing all this, I told him about my boss's anger and my feelings of guilt. His calm response was, "You were stuck and tried to get out. What else did he expect you to do?"

These words have stayed with me all through my career. One of my biggest satisfactions in life is helping people get unstuck and trying to give them the reassurance that tow truck driver gave me long ago.

He recognized that when people drive a lot, every once in a while, they get stuck. His job is to get them out – period. He didn't judge the person or the circumstances because that did nothing to help the situation.

I have met many people who are stuck. They spin their wheels by dealing with the same problem in the same way on a regular basis. I try not to judge that person or the situation. As I see it, my job is to give them a way out of the rut before the wheels fall off and start rolling down the highway.

The future Pies you make - Planning for major life events.

The *Life, By The Pie*™ process can also help you plan for major life events, major purchases, and significant lifestyle changes.

To illustrate how this can work, I will let someone very special to me tell you his story. Gordon Schmidt has been working on the *Life, By The Pie*™ program with me for the past six years. He developed the early Excel version of the program and he has used it in his own life and business for the past few years. Gordon is the first real user of the program. He has helped to make this concept of mine work. He is also a fine young man – someone I'm very proud to have as my partner in this great venture.

Here is Gordon's story:

A Financial Planner's Experience with Life, By The Pie™

It was several years ago, just after I had completed my Certified Financial Planner training when I worked for Michael Finkbeiner as a financial planner. I eagerly began working with clients using the latest and greatest in financial planning programs. Invariably I found that the program with all the bells and whistles focused on gimmickry instead of functionality and ultimately ended up missing the point. A financial plan is not something to be sold – it's supposed to serve a specific purpose.

I ended up asking all my clients a few simple questions. "What do you think a financial plan is?" and "What do you expect to gain from this process?"

My clients said a financial plan was something they absolutely believed they should have. But few of them had a clear goal – and a financial plan without a goal is useless. Once you have a goal, you need to know where you stand right now. This became problem number two – gathering the in-depth information needed to figure out those two things. The accuracy, and ultimately the efficacy of a financial plan are predicated on the accuracy of the information put into it.

It is during this period of information gathering that the financial planning process loses its luster. It becomes tedious and laborious and clients quickly begin to lose interest in the process, and if there isn't a clearly defined goal to begin with, the plan dies before it's created.

A financial plan is only as good as its implementation; if the process was tedious and laborious, then clients believe that the implementation will be just as difficult. This all combines to chip away at the drive to complete a financial plan. By the end of all the information gathering, I think clients were left feeling they had done all this work so that the person in the suit sitting across a desk – me – can justify selling them something they weren't sure they needed. The traditional financial planning process is fraught with frustration and disillusionment.

There are three main stages in a person's life: debt management, wealth accumulation, and retirement management. A financial plan is useful for all of these stages and more, but regardless of the purpose of the plan, you still need an accurate starting point. Whether you're planning for retirement or buying a new car, you need to know what your financial picture looks like *right now*. It was for these reasons that *Life, By The Pie*™ came into existence. It was financial planning in its purest form. All the superfluous material was cut to focus on the basics.

It was 2005 when Michael Finkbeiner called and told me about this incredible financial planning concept. That day I worked on creating a very simple worksheet on a database – a worksheet that would calculate taxes based on specific income types. It allows a user to keep track of all expenses, and all of them would be represented in a pie chart. The chart not only showed expenses, but showed them relative to income. It accounted for taxes. It showed financial decisions in their proper context.

At first I began using the worksheet on myself, simply to test its functionality. I quickly became reliant on it to manage my own finances. Knowing how much money I will make in a given year, I can use the worksheet to calculate roughly how much will go to taxes. What's left has to cover all my expenses. Most of my expenses, even the so-called variable expenses, are pretty much the same from year to year. Factoring in these amounts allows me to see how much income is left to cover all the expenses that I haven't accounted for.

The more I used the *Pie* system, the more accurate it became. Every time an expense came up that I hadn't previously thought of, I incorporated it into the worksheet. In the years that I have used the *Life, By The Pie*™ worksheet, I have been able to plan ahead for getting married to my incredible wife, the birth of our child and the prospect of buying a new house.

When we found out my wife was pregnant, we were overjoyed – but also nervous at the prospect of becoming parents. With all our trepidations about becoming first-time parents, we did not need the added stress of financial worry. We were going to need to make some relatively large purchases, like a crib. There were also going to be increased regular expenditures, like diapers and formula.

Using the *Life, By The Pie*™ worksheet allowed me to create a plan to fund the purchase of the big items. We also knew that when my wife went on maternity leave, we would simultaneously see a loss in total household income and an increase in regular expenses. The *Life, By The Pie*™ worksheet allowed me, first of all, to see if we would even have enough money coming in to cover the costs or if we would be running a deficit for that period of time. Secondly, I was able to create a budget that ultimately helped us get through that financially rough period without going into debt.

Some reading this may view what I have just written as being a very clinical depiction of such an immensely joyous event, but it was because I didn't have to worry about our finances that I was able to enjoy the experience more fully. Being in a position to know how much remaining income we have, takes a lot of stress away from financial decisions that may pop up from time to time. If you've ever wondered, "Can I afford this?", the *Life, By The Pie*™ worksheet can tell you.

Several months ago a house came on the market in a neighborhood my wife and I liked. Buying it seemed like it could be a good move. Naturally we wondered, "Can we afford it?" We turned to our *Life, By The Pie*™ worksheet to find out. Within a few minutes I was able to see our answer.

We entered in the prospective mortgage amount, property taxes and utilities and could clearly see that we would be able to afford it. We ultimately decided not to buy the house. We would have been able to afford it, but only if we sacrificed our travel budget in order to do it. At this stage in our lives, we value travel over homestead, and considering we love our current home, it wouldn't make sense for us to make the move.

Without the benefit of being able to see the whole picture, we would have run the calculations on a sheet of paper, which would have told us one thing... Yes, we can afford it. Without the context provided by the *Life, By The Pie*™ worksheet, we most likely would have purchased the house and dealt with a more limited ability to enjoy the things in life that give us the most pleasure.

Earlier I mentioned the three stages of life; I can tell you that I have and continue to use *Life, By The Pie*™ for all of these and much more. After all, it was never designed to be a gimmick to sell, it was designed to solve the problems associated with the reasons traditional financial planning failed. It was designed to show where my income is going and figure out how to achieve my financial goals.

For me personally, it works and I can't imagine managing my money and financial plans without it.

Major Life Events - Retirement

I don't think there is a more common major life event than retirement. We all have to retire to some degree, at some time in our lives.

Many pre-retired people struggle with how much money it takes to retire. If you listen to some sources, you would think it would take at least $1 million set aside for a totally fulfilled post-work life.

My experience has been that everyone needs different amounts of retirement income and only the individual can determine what is needed to make him or her happy. When it comes to retirement, there are three factors that matter:

1. When can you retire?
2. How much will you need to live on in retirement?
3. How much must be saved?

These factors are interrelated. If you know (a) when you want to retire and (b) how much you will need in retirement, I can tell you how much you have to save to do that.

OR

If I know (b) how much you need in retirement and (c) how much you can save, then I can tell you when you can retire.

OR

If you tell me (c) how much you can save and (a) when you want to retire, I can tell you how much you will have to live on.

This last option is the most common way people approach retirement. They know they want to get out of their current situation and they only have a certain amount saved. Then they're appalled at the reduction in their standard of living if they decide to go ahead and retire.

I find a lot of people focused on (a) without much thought about (b) and (c) – that is until it's too late.

My Slices

The *Life, By The Pie*™ process can help you figure out how much money you really need to feel happy and content on a regular basis by isolating and identifying those slices of your Pie. Sometimes this may require you to live on less and learn to be happy with what you've got. Sometimes you may have more money than you thought you did. I find that most people are pretty happy with what they have, but they've just never properly defined that amount.

Defining slices of the Pie that are for you versus slices that are given or paid to others is a very important exercise in determining how much it takes to make you happy. Attending the University of You will help you determine what it takes to make a fulfilling Pie for right now, and most likely in your retirement as well.

If you are approaching retirement, or the work afterlife as I like to call it, you are hopefully about to jettison some major expenses.

Some of the major components or slices of your Pie that may be changing or eliminated entirely are:

1. mortgage payments
2. support of children
3. work related expense

This list is not exhaustive, nor is it meant to be. It's just a simple list to help get you started considering what current expenses will be eliminated or reduced within a certain timeframe.

There are certain ingredients of your Pie that are important to you now and may always be important to you for the rest of your life. I know many people who have retired on much less than some financial minimum put out by a financial guru because they're doing the things that make them happy and they always have. They also have learned to live within their means.

The *Life, By The Pie*™ process can help you to determine (b) how much you will need to live on in retirement. It will also tell you (c) how much you can save because while you're living according to your true taste, you've learned to put enough aside. When you can retire (a) becomes very simple now that we know the first two factors.

If all this doesn't work for you, you will have to go through the exercise and change your spending patterns accordingly.

Remember, there is nothing wrong with working longer or in a different capacity. As you may remember, it wasn't too long ago that people were expected to work a lot longer than they do today. Somehow people seem to think they've failed if they can't be "free" of work at 55.

Another thing I want you to keep in mind is to be careful what you wish for. If you hate what you do for a living now, chances are you're not going to be ecstatically happy in retirement. I find a lot of my happily retired clients were pretty satisfied with life when they were working.

The same life skills that make you happy in one situation seem to somehow carry over to the next. Don't forget that no matter what circumstances change in the course of your life, you are the common element. Your attitude and your belief system have more to do with what makes you happy than any realities you perceive in your current situation.

Simply put, through all aspects of your life, you always take **you** with you.

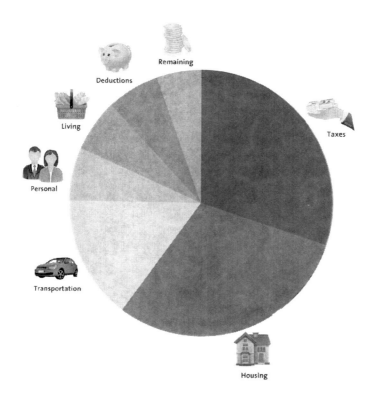

Activate Your Free
Life, By The Pie Account

As a thank you for purchasing this book you are entitled to a free *Life, By The Pie*™ account, good for one calendar year. Your account gives you access to the *Life, By The Pie*™ budgeting tool and our mobile expense tracker, The Daily Dish™. To receive your free account, use **FPFAV1NHMVS8** as your activation code when you visit the lifebythepie.com website.

About the Authors

For a Financial Advisor, **Michael Finkbeiner** has an interesting combination of training and life experiences. He majored in economics at the University of Western Ontario (BA), and has two designations in accounting (CGA) and retirement planning (RRC). He also has a certification in financial planning (PFP). The man should be a traditionalist when it comes to managing money.

Then you find out that he still competes in javelin. You just don't imagine a buttoned down financial guy throwing a spear all over the world for fun. Or having an off the wall sense of humour.

Michael has always been fascinated by how things work by the numbers, which triggered a lot of questioning. Especially when he saw how many people have trouble figuring out their life and financial goals, and how to achieve them.

He loves what he does, and he sees his job as helping clients achieve their dreams. Michael came up with the novel idea of looking at personal finances like a Pie. Not the pie chart that bored everyone to tears in his Statistics class at the university, but a Pie for life that had layers, depth, and flavour; a Pie as unique as the individual who created it.

Life, By The Pie™ and the website that is a companion tool, grew out of that idea. Michael has always been a story-teller. It's how he connects to people. His stories in this book will entertain you, but more importantly, help you connect with a new way to understand and manage your money.

Jan Dean is a journalist and freelance writer. With a B.A. and M.A. in early modern European history, she gravitated to business writing and then journalism for the pleasure of writing about people who are still alive.

She has the ability to get interested in just about anything that crosses her path. That explains her reading habit and library fines. Jan also loves to laugh, especially with her family.

CPSIA information can be obtained at www.ICGtesting.com
Printed in the USA
LVOW12s0526110614

389450LV00006B/15/P